STOP
DOING WHAT
YOU SHOULD

THE MILLENNIAL'S GUIDE TO NAVIGATING
YOUR MOST REWARDING CAREER PATH

WHITNEY K. BLAINE

STOP DOING WHAT YOU SHOULD

ISBN: 978-0692482223

CONTENTS

Dedication		*i*
Foreword by Tim Tessalone		*iii*
Prologue		*1*
1	What is "Should"?	7
2	Define Your Skill Set	23
3	Be Unorthodox	35
4	Excel at Listening	79
5	Determine Your Fate	89
6	Be a Great Colleague	117
7	Live in Intuition	129
8	Take the Plunge	143
9	One-Off "Shoulds"	151

DEDICATION

FOR THE FIRST TIME in my life, I am at a loss for words. Appreciation, gratitude, and thankfulness are words that describe how I feel for the dozens of people who made an impact on my life and on this book, but they just don't seem to be enough.

First, I dedicate this book to my parents, Davis and Karen, for without their love and encouragement, I wouldn't have had the strength to write it. They always remind me of my passion and skill, even if I forever lament to them that I'll never be a Hemingway or Whitman.

To my mentors Tim, Jacob, Kim, Charlie, Bob, Samira, and Dan: I continue to dip into your wells of knowledge, and you never let me down or turn me away. Also, I want to give thanks to the countless number of people I've met in the past decade who have shared their anecdotes or experiences. Thank you for the endless knowledge and providing me with another perspective.

To my siblings Justin, Tristan, and Brittara: You played a pivotal role in pushing me to be better than I thought I could. Thank you.

To my friends, who have allowed me to bounce ideas off of them over the years: Thanks for the endless support, and for never suggesting that writing a book at age 25 "wasn't cool." To Dave, who helped me realize that I can accomplish whatever I aspire to: thank you.

And to all the young people who have ever asked to pick my brain or requested a meeting with me: Thank you for challenging me and forcing
me to question my methods. You are the inspiration for this book, and I
only hope you get as much out of it as I have from writing it.

FOREWORD

WHEN YOU CONSIDER the path of Whitney Blaine's nascent career, you might think it is paradoxical that she has authored a book full of career advice.

After all, she is already onto her fourth job, and she hasn't even left her 20s.

But that's the VERY REASON why no one is more relevant than Whitney to tell her peers to "Stop Doing What You Should." Because despite what it seems, she has been doing exactly the right thing in her young career: finding HER happiness and not somebody else's. Or, as she says in one of the later chapters of this book, "Live your life the way you imagined it, not the way others say you should."

The transition from college into the work force is daunting. I've always felt that this is the most challenging time of a person's life, as one determines his/her career path with their first (or fourth in Whitney's case) job. As the father of three post-college kids navigating their ways through young adulthood and the workforce, I know these struggles first-hand.

Finding that job—or that right job—is not an easy process. In this book, Whitney breaks that difficult process down in terms that are eye-opening and direction-setting to millennials.

The interview and workplace etiquette Whitney suggests in *Stop Doing What You Should* might seem evident to those of us with years of experience in the workplace. But as someone who has heard from hundreds of job seekers, you'd be amazed how often applicants fail to "check off" the simple things, like proofreading an email, posting appropriately on social media, showing respect, or even saying thank you.

"...gleaning the wisdom imparted in this book is a smart investment in your future."

She also has perceptive tips on how to network to find a job, how to grab an employer's attention when you are seeking a specific job, how to be a great co-worker once you acquire that job, and how to grow as you progress through your job. I especially loved her "talk to strangers" advice (my old parenting mantra be damned!) to help make connections and gain life knowledge; what better example puts this book's title into context?

Whitney tells you how to make an impression, why you need to listen more than talk, and, perhaps most importantly, why you must trust your intuition. She also tells you how to leave a job—or career—that turns out not to be right for you. Remember, she has "been there" several times.

Whitney eloquently combines her thoughts and advice in such a cogent and organized manner, sprinkling in real-life anecdotes that she has either lived or witnessed. I am delighted that she is willing to share this intel in order to assist others.

So, if you are entering the job market for the first time, or transitioning from your first job to your next, or even if you are coming from a more experienced viewpoint, then gleaning the wisdom imparted in this book is a smart investment in your future. Before you fill out that on-line employment application or send in your résumé to that appealing job opportunity, take the time to read this book...carefully. You'll not only gain a big advantage over the many other applicants competing with you for that position, you also won't be left saying many years from now, "I wish I knew then what I know now."

Go ahead, you have my permission, and Whitney's: Stop doing what you should...except for reading this book—you should be doing that!

— Tim Tessalone, USC Sports Information Director.
Tim has mentored hundreds of people, providing years of career advice, throughout his tenure as the media relations liaison for USC Athletics.

PROLOGUE

I **WASN'T AWARE** that I lived an unorthodox life until recently. Over the years, I recognized I was, on occasion, a bit bolder than my friends and probably took a couple more risks than the average person. But, it was not until I started climbing that proverbial ladder of success when I fully grasped that my approach to life was rather unique.

As I made my way through college and into a couple of better-than-average jobs, I made decisions that seemed to puzzle others who would commonly ask, "How did you do that" or "Where did you get that idea from?"

More often than not, I didn't know how to quell their disbelief. The words "you're lucky" got tossed around quite a bit. To that end, I would reply with some form of "I do this or that because it's what I know." It was certainly a vague response, but it sufficed to shorten a potentially lengthy conversation about all the extra steps I had taken over the years to take advantage of any possible opportunity. And truthfully, I strategically made certain decisions throughout my personal and professional life because it was what I had to do to *stand out.*

And while I'm still in the early stages of my career (and haven't reached nearly a fraction of the success I desire), I knew I was onto something with my approach because it continued to reap dividends for both myself and my friends. Unlike many others who are reliant on the advice or guidance of others, I found personal happiness through my professional methodology because I sought results on my own terms.

Because of the bold approach I've taken to life, all sorts of people have asked me for advice. When prompted, I'd share a tip here or there. Since I was a teenager—when one could argue I didn't have any advice to give—these kinds of conversations became commonplace. Most of this early advice was simply an accumulation of other people's life experiences that I heard and remembered. As I began to experience my own professional stumbles and "wins," I added these learnings to the stories others provided me. Eventually, the amount of pooled advice became substantial; it was more than could be shared over a cup of coffee.

That is how this book came to life. I want you to reap the dividends of my collected experiences, so you can apply them to your own life. There are infinite career resources around, but I have yet to stumble upon one source that provides millennials with as relevant a perspective. Hopefully you find that the tips discussed in this text provide a practical overview, while getting rid of all the clutter.

So, how can you approach your career in a way that stands out among the pack? How will you reach your own professional and personal happiness, even if you can't imagine what that looks like yet? The answer is by achieving results on your own terms.

The opinions of others are seemingly inescapable. So often we want to do things on our own terms while receiving the approval of everyone else. Those are separate desires, and rarely happen in accord with one another. And that's probably the biggest hurdle we face when taking action: overcoming the judgment of others. We need to remind our-selves that our actions are ours alone; the approval of others is merely a by-product of those actions.

See what happens if you step outside the "box" others have created for you, and instead create your own. Why? Why not. What's the worst that can happen...if nothing happens? The result of our action is not inaction—or worse, moving backward. We don't need a perfect out-come to glean substance or value from our choices. If nothing else, the value is derived from a choice that was totally and completely ours!

"So often we want to do things on our own terms while receiving the approval of everyone else. Those are separate desires, and rarely happen in accord with one another."

Realistically, reaching professional and personal happiness can be a long, painstaking process. Sometimes, we think it happens overnight. Let's say you get married and land the job of your dreams within the same week. There is no doubt your life is great at that point. But a couple months later, your smile disappears as the harsh realities of life become more apparent: You need to find a house that you can't af-ford, your new boss turns out to be a jerk, you are buried in work that is not exactly what you wanted or imagined, and so forth.

Happiness is fluid; it feels omnipresent when life events occur, yet it feels like a stranger when we're trying to surmount obstacles over which we seem to have no control. When we do have control over these obstacles—when we can take a weekend job to save some money for that mortgage or approach our boss about the best way he or she can maximize our work productivity—the lows don't feel as low.

It's difficult to feel total satisfaction when we've been coerced into choices or aren't entirely aware of who actually made our decisions. When we listen to the advice of others or seek out external opinions, people commonly use the word "should" to lead us down a specific path. But that path isn't always our direct road to success.

Ever hear someone say, "You should do so and so, because that's just how the system works?" Or they say, "You should do this and that, because [insert name here] did, and look where they are now?" While people's suggestions can be valuable and help you gain perspective, to blindly follow someone's advice is not always the best course of action.

The wonderfully brilliant writer Hunter S. Thompson once wrote to a friend on this same topic:

> To give advice to a man who asks what to do with his life implies something very close to egomania. To presume to point a man to the right and ultimate goal—to point with a trembling finger in the RIGHT direction is something only a fool would take upon himself.[1]

In my personal and professional life, I have heeded the advice of others. I've done the "should" and the "have-to's." At times, these suggested tactics are simply necessary—instances where a "SHOULD"

---

becomes a "MUST" (to be discussed further in the following chapter)—and we just have to suck it up and do the damned thing. But if you employ the tactics and approaches I discuss throughout this book, you'll be able to better distinguish an essential piece of "should" advice from generic advice that might not apply to or enhance your life.

My approach isn't revolutionary. Truth is, anyone can do what I do. And it's not systematic, either. Rather, my method is a compilation of tactics, some or all of which may resonate with you, including:

- How to change careers early in your professional life

- How to build meaningful relationships in today's modern, uber-connected world by disposing of the traditional way we think of "networking"

- How to strategically apply to desirable jobs, including how to make your résumé stand out from the competition

- How to engage "strangers" and increase your network by welcoming new contacts and learning opportunities

- How to determine your individual value and skill set

- How to earn professional respect, no matter your age, gender, or lack of experience

Regardless of where you are in life or what your path may be, the goal of this book is to equip you with enough unique tools to propel you toward professional satisfaction.

But after reading this book, you will eventually have to stop talking or thinking about these strategies and actually apply them. You'll have to go out and take the actions yourself. Otherwise, you're just following the path of everyone else, heeding inordinate amounts of generic advice without discerning what tactics specifically resonate and work for you.

If you read this book and decide to apply some of the tactics described herein, I don't know what your future will look like. Your actions are and will be completely different from whatever actions I or others have likely taken. There is no formula or science to success. Our future is up for discovery. But that's the beauty behind it all: *Whatever happens in your life is a result of your actions alone.* Nobody else can take full credit for your path. And while I give partial credit to a few select mentors for my "success" (it's all relative, right?), I still had to go out and take the actions myself. But I feel satisfaction and progress every day because my choices and actions—including the mistakes—I made alone.

Ultimately, I believe anyone can train his or herself to follow a similar approach to what is outlined in this book. Because there's really only one rule to follow:

Stop Doing What You Should.

CHAPTER ONE

WHAT IS "SHOULD"?

*"The only good thing to do with good advice is pass it on;
it is never of any use to oneself."*

— Oscar Wilde

" **S**HOULD" SEEMS LIKE a pretty ordinary word at the outset. But as I've received much advice over the years, I ultimately realized that the word "should" has a rather offensive connotation. Think about how the word is used. People typically employ or imply "should" in one of several ways, including:

- as a threshold for comparison (i.e., "this person did so and so to get to this point, so we should, too")

- because of precedence (i.e., "that's how it should be done because that's how it's always been done")

- to delineate something (i.e., "we should just wait our turn")

The word "should" simply reeks of judgment and subjection. If we don't do what someone suggests we "should," or we take a different approach, we're not likely to receive this person's approval. The word is quite a paradox. When someone uses "should," he or she is often suggesting that there is a specific or appropriate path to achieving something great. But, at the same time, if we are following the same suggested path that everyone else is taking, the likelihood of achieving something "great" is actually not that likely; we've simply become one of many, and nowhere near where we "should" be at all.

WHEN TO ADHERE TO "SHOULD"

You can probably gather that I have a negative opinion of the word "should." Hopefully, you will soon join me in my revolution against the term. But first, I need to acknowledge instances in which *adhering* to "should" is actually beneficial, and critical to our professional advancement. With that said, here are a few things we SHOULD absolutely and unequivocally do:

- **Avoid "Holding Words."** I didn't listen to my dad often as a kid, but when I did, he always said I took too long to tell a story. Initially, this hurt my feelings, because I didn't understand why I could not keep his attention. As I got older, I noticed I unintentionally peppered my stories with the words "um" and "like." I now refer to these as "holding words," meaning they drag out or hold up one's story (or talking point). Holding words can also: affect the listener's attention span, minimize the speaker's central point, or make the storyteller appear unconfident.

  The ability to tell stories well or clearly communicate an idea is useful to any career. Not only does a good communicator appear confident and professional, but an extremely talented storyteller also has the power to influence others, often relating to a broad spectrum of people. There is only a handful of people I consider "great" storytellers. My oldest brother Justin—although he's not without his flaws—is one of them. Justin can effectively tell a story by including only the relevant details that enhance or build up to his central point. He can play to his audience well, accordingly shifting his tone or adjusting his verbiage. Still, the most impressive part of his skill is that he never uses a holding word. Without any filler, his stories seem to flow at a quick clip and are almost always engaging (except when they involve his little sister).

While it seems obvious that one should avoid these holding words whenever possible, I don't think many advisors or mentors provide this guidance to young people. Frankly, it can be uncomfortable calling someone out when he or she says "like" or "um" too often. Most people are already self-conscious about the way they present themselves, especially in their teens and 20s. Those older than us probably assume that our communication skills will improve as we gain professional experience. Personally, I prefer to be told immediately if I'm doing something that could potentially impact my job performance, even if hearing it can be uncomfortable in that moment. When I am providing someone with advice, and I hear an excessive amount of "um" or "like" woven into his or her sentences, I suggest a practice that worked for me: Talk in front of a mirror about a subject you don't know well. Most people are able to easily discuss topics in which they already feel knowledgeable.

But the practice of speaking on a subject that we feel less confident about is a great way to slow down our story, and hopefully we can eventually reduce the use of these holding words.

Here's an example of how this practice worked for a "mentee" of mine: I met Heather in the beginning of her junior year. She came to me with no clear idea of her career path but could not explain why she was so confused. She took internships in talent acquisition (a fancy word for "human resources" at many companies) and event coordination, and even expressed an inclination to work in sports. I suggested she keep her options open while continuing to hone her skills at whatever internship she was offered, rather than be caught up on the field itself. The trouble was that, because she was so confused on her path, she wasn't able to articulate in interviews why she wanted the specific position or internship. Even in our weekly phone conversations, she used holding words because she thought she needed an answer for everything. I assured her that many people also don't know where they're going to end up, but that uncertainty shouldn't prevent her from speaking confidently about how she got to this point. She now practices removing holding words from her speech by discussing the day's news in front of a mirror. As each week progressed, I noticed her decreased use of holding words, and a generally more refined disposition.

- **Express Humility.** I provide career advice to countless graduates or soon-to-be graduates throughout the calendar year. The meetings range from informational interviews, to brief phone calls on a particular topic, to simply doing a one-off favor for a friend's son or daughter (e.g., editing a résumé). If I have the time, and someone asks, I never mind meeting or providing advice. After all, I often request meetings with people older than I, so why wouldn't I do the same for those younger?

Unfortunately, many of the people I've spoken with feel as though the available jobs they've encountered are somehow beneath them, or they're overqualified for them. Some young people have a tendency to say they are already "experienced" in a particular area. If you haven't worked in the real world yet, you aren't experienced. Not a knock on you, that's just the reality of your situation. I have been out of college for four years, and I acknowledge that my experience is still limited.

Or, the opposite of overconfidence occurs and someone tells me they get incredibly nervous in interviews or conversations. When this is the case, I often suggest conducting a mock interview. The goal of this exercise is to prepare someone to get rid of his or her butterflies. Upon "entering" the fictitious room, I (acting as the hiring manager) ask the person simply to talk about him or herself. More often than not, these mock interviews become a conversation about how he or she is great at X, Y, and Z. Those qualities are nice to know, but they don't explain how this person can add value to the company. Without context, they simply list off their array of talents, which – even if they feel nervous and insecure on the inside – can appear boastful to an outsider. Most companies are concerned with their bottom line, so be strategic when interviewing. Focus on how your skills fit the given role, thus advancing the larger organization.

Whether you're inexperienced or overqualified, nothing will impact you or your career as much as the impression you leave with somebody. Expressing humility is critical to your long-term future. No matter the stage of your career, you must speak to everyone you encounter as if they have the same amount of life experience and knowledge. "Gratitude" and "humility" are two character traits that will forever be a "should." Even if someone tells you something you already knew or heard previously, perhaps act like it was the first time you've heard the information; your contact may be more likely to make a further investment in you if they believe they are contributing to your growth and you appreciate their time.

"Whether you're inexperienced or overqualified, nothing will impact you or your career as much as the impression you leave with somebody."

- **Follow Up With Others.** This "should" is applicable across all industries and people. It is a widely accepted rule that one must message a contact following a conversation. So, no matter whom you meet, for how long, when, or where—always follow up. Even if you are swamped, set a reminder in your phone to send a quick thank you note.

Remember how I said I hate the word "should"? Well, I love it in this context because I wholeheartedly believe that sending a follow-up note (typically within a week of any meeting) is a "must-do" for everyone, at any level. Even if the conversation wasn't particularly enjoyable, or useful, you "should" *still* send a follow-up note.

Following up with others may have a significantly positive impact on your career:

- First, it gets you into the habit of appreciating when others give you their time. Time is very valuable to each of us, so it is important not to take someone's time for granted. Remember, your contact could have spent his or her time talking to someone else.

- Second, which is essentially an extension of my first point, a follow-up note quite literally indicates your appreciation. If you are thanking someone for taking the time to meet with you, then they know you appreciated it. Still, the note must be written and the thanks must be said.

- Third, a follow-up note is a great opportunity to remind the person about you. If the person takes informationals or meetings of this kind often, then he or she may forget about you, or isn't able to differentiate you from "Joe" who sent a similar email last week. Use this email as a chance to indicate something special about the meeting you had. If you stumbled upon a shared interest, or your contact mentioned a good piece of material, recall that in the

message. Research the item in advance of your email so
you can demonstrate your ability to see things through to
completion.

- **Actively Listen.** Pardon the generalization, but millennials tend
to be poor listeners. While not universally applicable to all those
that ascribe to Generation Y, it is commonly acknowledged—
even by millennials themselves—that young people tend to be
more easily distracted. In a 2013 survey by JWTIntelligence,
nearly 70 percent of millennials claimed they wanted to learn
how to improve their focus.[2] As the first generation to be raised
completely in the digital age, we grew up multi-tasking.

Whether these interferences are within our immediate line of
sight or in the background—we constantly encounter, snooze,
and mute various alerts that pop up on our phones or beep from
our computer screens. We're always *semi*-tuned in. As a member
of the Generation, I can honestly admit that it can be difficult
determining when something might actually be meaningful or
if that thing is just a time-zapper.

However, if you can give your undivided attention to another,
active listening becomes your advantage in the marketplace.
You automatically differentiate yourself from your peers when
you are fully engaged in someone else. Beyond simply *appearing*
focused to that person, the major benefit of actively listening
to another is the actual value that can be derived from learning
about others' shared experiences.

---

[2] www.bbc.com/capital/story/20150408-a-generation-of-cyberslackers

That said, taking meetings and listening to as many people as you can is another acceptable "should." What better way to practice and develop your active listening skills? Similar to sending a follow-up note, taking and requesting meetings will benefit you at any age. Over time, the accumulation of these in-person meetings will undoubtedly provide you with invaluable perspective. So, while the majority of our generation likely spends an inordinate amount of time succumbing to our social media news feeds, you instead are learning and planning for your future.

- **Proofread Written Communications.** This one seems like a no brainer, but you might be surprised. I can't tell you how many interns I have managed or supervised who frequently misspelled words. We all have access to the spell check button; there's little excuse for misspelling. I've also had bosses who spell or use words incorrectly in emails, and it is akin to seeing an elephant in the meeting room; everyone else recognizes that this person isn't a sufficient communicator. Simple mistakes in professional communications instantly cause someone to lack credibility, no matter his or her seniority. People often question someone's ability and position in the workplace when his or her communications are frequently littered with misspelled words and grammatical errors.

If you received a college degree, you know that spelling incorrectly would have led to poor marks in class. Why not apply the same logic to your career, but replacing a potentially bad grade with your boss' poor evaluation of you? At the same time, spelling correctly and using appropriate grammar are skills that people notice *when done well*. While most written communications occur in email these days, you can still showcase that degree you worked so hard for and apply your strong communication skills over email. If you choose not to, frequent errors in your emails may lead one to assume you are:

A. not taking this particular task or the person you're addressing very seriously

B. too bogged down with work to give the email another glance

C. lazy.

None of the aforementioned is a good trait or assumption for another to have about you; so, just spell correctly, for goodness sake!

Here's an example to illustrate further the importance of this "should": An intern I managed once incorrectly spelled the last name of one of our company executives. But that little squiggly red line denoting a misspelled word in spell check didn't appear because the incorrect word she used was an actual word in the dictionary—it just wasn't a very appropriate word, or one too many people commonly use. My boss not only scolded the intern but she was also then perceived as insensitive and immature because of one incorrectly spelled word! Do your homework and double-check the accurate spelling of peoples' names. For an extremely difficult name, write it down several times so it becomes more familiar. The few minutes you spend ensuring you get it right could save you months you might otherwise spend trying to correct a mistake.

- **Maintain Appropriate Social Media Profiles.** This is the ultimate "should." Whether it's a tweet that could be misconstrued or a picture posted of a girl in a skimpy bikini surrounded by guys and alcohol, sharing this kind of content isn't beneficial for any professional. Frankly, looking at inappropriate social media profiles is rather painful; it's like these people have unlocked a window for us to peer into their private lives. Even if your profile is private, people can save images and find ways of obtaining your personal information online. If someone is motivated enough, anybody can see what you are interested in, who you are following, and where you go.

I like to envision every picture or status I post as a permanent stamp of my brand. I imagine my published content lives on forever, even outliving me, because it probably does. With posts I'm apprehensive about publishing, my rule of thumb is this: rather than say or show something now that I may not be proud of in a decade, I am better serving my future self by being silent. It's kind of like the social media golden rule, if you will. For example, if you're in your 20s and frequently take trips to Las Vegas, you might want to keep those memories in your mental bank for fear of setting a bad example to your future kids, or having an image used against you in the midst of a future parenting lesson. Imagine if social media existed in your parents' heyday; hopefully any momentary revulsion you just felt will make you rethink any content you plan to publish. Also, everyone is easily searchable these days. I know first-hand. I worked as a reporter and stumbled upon aspects of people in my research that I wish I had not seen. The Internet will last a lot longer than we ever will, so let's clean up our profiles before we embarrass not just ourselves and our kids, but maybe even their kids!

Here's an example of social media affecting someone's position at work: A former colleague of mine paid great attention to her appearance in the office. She wore tall stiletto heels, lots of makeup, and possessed extreme confidence. One day, I found a couple of my male colleagues all huddled around. I walked over to them and said, "What are you guys going on about?" Sure enough, they were looking at my female colleague's Instagram profile, as she had posted some extremely revealing photos of herself earlier that day. Within that circle of men was someone who had the power to promote her. It has been a few years since I've worked at that company, but I am fairly certain she has the same title to this day.

- **Stay Informed.** Whether it's reading about current events or emerging trends in your industry, be aware of what is going on around you. If you don't constantly consume content, you are essentially handing someone else your golden ticket. You may think you're strapped for time and can't keep up with all available information. And you probably can't. But that doesn't mean you shouldn't try to consume *some* of it. Subscribe to email newsletters that recap the biggest news of the day or detail innovative developments in your given field. You can turn on the radio and listen to the news in your car, or download a mobile app for news.

You can even subscribe to various Facebook pages that provide updated information. There is absolutely no reason you can't stay up-to-date on current events and issues.

Another reason to stay informed—aside from the knowledge you gain—is that doing so enhances your ability to connect with others. Whether it's a good book, new music, or random news, staying abreast of current trends and events gives you social currency. You can bridge new conversation with all sorts of people when you have something interesting or potentially valuable to say.

WHEN TO ADHERE TO "SHOULD"

AVOID "HOLDING WORDS" • ACTIVELY LISTEN • STAY INFORMED • EXPRESS HUMILITY

FOLLOW UP WITH OTHERS • MAINTAIN APPROPRIATE SOCIAL MEDIA PROFILES • PROOFREAD WRITTEN COMMUNICATIONS

WHEN TO **ABOLISH** "SHOULD"

Hopefully, all of the aforementioned "shoulds" are reasonable enough that you're doing them already. If you do all those things, you will undoubtedly get a job somewhere. If you also act kindly and have decent work experience, you will likely land on your feet and have a fine career.

But who wants to be just fine these days? Don't you want to excel? After seeing many of our grandparents and parents work tirelessly just to survive, rather than work in occupations they were passionate about, shouldn't we try to avoid that kind of life?

There are a number of discouraging attributes of our generation, but there are also some remarkable ones. Our will is one such example. We recognize our intrinsic abilities and are optimistic that we can accomplish whatever we set out to do. Our grandparents and parents might have recognized their unique capabilities, too, but they did not have the same range of professional choice that we do today. So, while we can go through the motions and clock in and out of our jobs in monotony, is that really how we want to live our lives?

To be extraordinary—or to accomplish goals you never thought you could—you have to take a different path than the rest. You need to separate yourself from those who constantly follow and adhere to "should." So, how is this idea manifested? The general guideline I use is: When it makes absolute sense, follow the advice of others. The rest of the time, follow your own intuition.

We accept a certain number of "shoulds" in our careers, because not adhering to them puts us at a disadvantage. A more apt term in these instances is probably "must-dos," but you get the point nonetheless. However, beyond those particular "shoulds" or "must-dos," it becomes unclear when to re-label a "should" as a personal "should not." At what point do we stop accepting how people generally perceive success, and start looking at our careers individually, through our own lens, path, and experiences? That time is **now**.

By abolishing "should" in most cases, we are certainly taking a leap of faith. My sincere hope is that the tactics described in this book make that leap look a little less frightening, and more like a hop, onto your next destination.

In order to be different, you have to think differently. I'm probably telling you something you already *know*, but maybe you don't *know how*. Realistically, the act of being different will manifest itself differently within each person. The best way to "be different" is by applying certain tactics to your life, which enable you to start thinking in an unorthodox way.

Throughout this book, I will provide many suggestions (typically an action I have previously taken or something I have seen) that have produced at least mild success. I have also included tactics or ideas that I applied or witnessed that proved a deterrent in my personal quest for professional happiness.

Perhaps you will not find my advice or suggestions helpful, or applicable to you and your career. Maybe applying these unorthodox tools won't work for you or enhance your life. At the very least, hopefully knowing these different approaches exist can help you determine what *doesn't* work for you.

I don't have all the answers. Nor do I pretend to. I have some—and from the advice I've given to people over the last few years, I have witnessed some fairly positive results. But this book is only meant to serve as a guide; take it at face value, and allow it to inform and enhance your professional path.

In no way **should** you follow my lead alone. You **should**, however, follow your own.

CHAPTER TWO

DEFINE YOUR SKILL SET

*"Rest satisfied with doing well,
and leave others to talk of you as they please."*

- Pythagoras

YOU'RE NOT GOING to be liked by everyone—a harsh, but true, reality. Excuse my brief philosophizing, but there is an important concept to accept (or acknowledge) before continuing into the meat of this book: The perceptions of others might subconsciously affect the decisions you make or actions you take, potentially preventing you from doing something you actually want.

I'll refer to Thompson once more, as he illustrates this idea of individual choice so eloquently, pulling from Shakespeare to demonstrate his point:

> *"To be, or not to be: that is the question: Whether 'tis nobler in the mind to suffer the slings and arrows of outrageous fortune, or to take arms against a sea of troubles…"*

> *And indeed, that IS the question: whether to float with the tide, or to swim for a goal. It is a choice we must all make consciously*

*or unconsciously at one time in our lives. So few people under-
stand this! Think of any decision you've ever made, which had
a bearing on your future: I may be wrong, but I don't see how it
could have been anything but a choice, however indirect, between
the two things I've mentioned: the floating or the swimming.*[3]

So long as you are your biggest advocate, what others think will never
hold as much weight as your own opinion. Unconditionally prioritizing
you—including your wishes, actions, and choices—is an important
concept to adopt, especially as it relates to your career and professional aspirations.

Remember the title of this book: *Stop Doing What You Should*. Others
can and will always suggest the appropriate way of doing something.
However, I firmly believe if you just *do you*, everything else will fall into
place just the way it *should*.

"Doing you" isn't very clear-cut for some people, as it is an intangible
approach. It also isn't easy to maintain over time. Identifying what
makes us us (the essence of "doing you") takes a great deal of time
and introspection, and a fair amount of soul-searching. The benefit is
worth the cost, however, when you exhibit an output of confidence and
self-awareness that others in your industry assuredly lack (even if the
irony is that this approach is meant for you to better yourself, without
comparison to anyone else).

So do a little research into you. It's okay to take some time, as you
determine what your own path to professional and personal happiness
looks like. In fact, this time of reflection may be the most important
thing you could ever do for your career.

---

[3] www.brainpickings.org/2013/11/04/hunter-s-thomspon-letters-of-note-advice

I "did me" by quitting my job—more than once. The first time, I quit the industry in which I thought I'd work forever and moved across the country. I had a rising career as a journalist, but at some point along my upward trajectory, I realized I was simply going through the motions. Rather than maximizing my skills or expanding my interests, I succumbed to this feeling of complacency, and felt suffocated by it. So, I quit and moved to New York City with one suitcase and zero friends. But before my big move, I spent about two months searching for my path to professional happiness. Because I traveled often for work, I was able to save up quite a bit. I moved back home with my parents so I didn't accumulate any extraneous expenses. During this off time, I did "nothing" except ponder my life situation and state of mind (interspersed with a good amount of yoga). Honestly, I still search for happiness every day, as I continue to refine my goals and evolve as a person. But at that time in my life, comprehensive introspection was crucial to getting me to my next point. And even though I did "nothing" in the literal sense, it was my most productive two months ever.

I would not have the confidence I do today without self-searching. And I would never be able to "do me" as well as I do today if I wasn't able to admit my failings and grow from them.

This kind of introspection can help anybody, even if you already possess self-confidence. By examining yourself, including what you offer to the marketplace, you can hone in on two extremely valuable and differentiating assets. I call these your "back pocketers," or aspects of yourself which you can recall anytime. Essentially, these character discoveries are sitting in your figurative "back pocket" should an opportunity arise (e.g., a job interview, business call, or casual conversation).

DEFINING YOUR SKILL SET

The first of these two back pocketers is **defining your skill set**. What do you like to do? What do you want to do? What are you good at? What aren't you good at? A "skill set" in this context has a different definition than our common conception of the term, which is limited to one's capabilities. Here, it is referred to as the combination of your strengths *and interests*. While you may not be great at everything that interests you, when you have passion for something, you're more likely to be better at it – because you're likely to work on the skill anyway. On the other hand, if you possess a skill but lack passion for it, e.g. "being good with numbers while hating math," you are less likely to advance your skill because you have little motivation to improve.

Here's an example of a skill I developed purely out of motivation: I did not consider writing a part of my skill set until late in my teenage years. Truthfully I didn't like it much before that time. In high school I was the student who avoided papers until the last minute. Although I wasn't awful at it, my skill was nothing to write home about (pun intended). It wasn't until my freshman year in college when my perspective changed. While I entered school intending to major in neuroscience, one of my prerequisites was a series of writing intensives. Despite initially receiving poor grades in the course, I loved the way I could express myself within the parameters of the assignment. While I wanted to improve my grade to maintain my GPA, I also wanted to perform better because I thoroughly enjoyed the act of writing and improving this skill. Eventually, my grades improved, and by the end of my first year, I realized I not only wanted to be a "good" writer, I wanted to be one of the best. So I transferred colleges to attend a school that was highly regarded for its writing program. And while writing is a part of my skill set now, I spent years cultivating my ability. Because I wanted to be better, I took every chance I could to write more. I improved at a faster rate than I otherwise would have had I just wanted to receive a passing grade in that class.

To those who are still discovering or identifying their skill sets, it's worth noting that your collective skill set will likely evolve (as it did with my writing skill). What you thought you were once good at could be drastically different today if you haven't practiced it, or some life event occurred that caused you to become disinterested in one skill and more interested in another. If this sounds like you, and your skill set has evolved, you may be more open-minded to exploring new passions and interests as you've grown. That's a part of introspection - identifying if your skills have evolved, and discovering what your current skill set is at any given time. When you are always aware of your core strengths, you increase your possibility of leveraging those skills, either now or in the future. On the other hand, if you are keenly aware of the instances when your passions and capabilities collide, your skill set is probably already in your "back pocket." You may just need to fine-tune it.

Why is it important to have your skill set readily available? For starters, this knowledge breeds self-confidence. Possessing self-confidence allows one to feel more capable in the job market and in the midst of interviews. Also, when you know what you're good at and what you like to do, you can better determine the right (or wrong) job fit. You are more likely to gravitate toward positions that align to your skill set when you are more likely to succeed in those roles. According to Gallup,

people who use their strengths every day are six times more likely to
be engaged on the job.[1] If a role is not tailored to your strengths, do not
squeeze a square peg into a round hole. The chances are you won't like
the job or be as capable at it as someone else whose skills better align.

---

*"When you are continuously aware
of your core strengths, you increase
your possibility of leveraging those
skills, either now or in the future."*

Perhaps you aren't that introspective. Or, you've spent some time
soul-searching and still can't glean any insight into your strengths or
what you really want from life. Ask your closest friends and family members which activities seem to make you the happiest. Separately, write
down what you enjoy. Combine what you've learned from your family
with your own exploration. You'll likely end up with some overlap, which
is a pretty good starting point to help narrow down a few core interests.

Another helpful approach is taking a formal personality or strengths
test. One I have experience using and recommend is the Clifton
StrengthsFinder, which is an online assessment that provides your top
five strengths for $10. If you'd like to determine additional strengths
(such as your bottom five, which one could also consider weaknesses),
there are incremental costs associated. As for a personality test, the
Meyers-Briggs Type Indicator (MBTI) is probably the most well-known.
Rather than detail your strengths or indicate your skill set, the MBTI

---

[1] www.gallup.com/businessjournal/155036/embedding-strengths-company-dna.aspx

is helpful in providing a list of careers common to your ascribed personality type. Here are a few other tests I've heard about (but cannot confirm their legitimacy):

- Strengths Tests: VIA Survey, RichardStep Strengths and Weaknesses Aptitude Test (RSWAT)

- Personality Tests: DiSC test, 16PF, Enneagrams

Still, a couple of cautions to take when considering this type of resource:

1. One, most formal assessments employ their own vernacular. These tests are usually created by psychologists and/or scientists, so the output isn't something you could automatically flip for use in an interview.

   - For instance, according to StrengthsFinder, my five strengths are: Achiever, Responsibility, Competition, Activator, Maximizer. If a hiring manager asks me what I'm good at, I would never respond "activating." That just doesn't make sense. Now, upon further reading, the test's description of its "Activator" category says I am impatient for action and that I believe action is the best mechanism for learning. Looking internally, I would agree with both of those statements. A more colloquial way of reiterating this strength to someone else would probably be "proactive."

2. Second, these tests categorize a wide range of people. While they attempt to provide an individual assessment based on your specific answers, remember that there are hundreds or possibly thousands of people taking this same test. If something seems

either a bit too generic or not entirely applicable to you, don't spend too long thinking about it. After all, you know yourself best. This resource is most helpful when thought of as a supplementary guide. Hopefully it will provide you with a better frame of reference or confirm your initial thoughts, but the results should never change your view of yourself (unless you recognize a weakness that you'd like to change).

Also, knowing your skill set helps to overshadow any conversation about your perceived weaknesses. Often stated as, "What are your expected areas of development," there are a couple of ways to answer this loaded question:

1. Provide one or two traits that you're consciously trying to improve upon, while adding helpful context to these "weaknesses." Perhaps you lack the skill because you never had the opportunity to work on it, whether in school or at a previous job. **The key to this approach is stressing your optimism and openness to developing additional experience in this area, especially if it is critical to performing well in a given role.** Thus, despite a potentially underdeveloped skill set, in your desire to be better, you're displaying an upside to hiring you.

    –   One caution with this tactic: ensure you aren't making excuses or placing blame when you acknowledge where you can improve. The reason why you didn't get the opportunity to develop this skill isn't important; just state that you didn't. If you are prodded further, one potential exit out of the question is stating that your previous job required you to prioritize other skills.

2. Tailor your weaknesses to one or two traits that you suspect aren't essential to the position. For example, maybe you are not the most adept in math. That may be a totally acceptable weakness if you're applying for a communications position. If you're trying to get a job in operations or analysis, however, maybe avoid mentioning those poor math skills. Instead, emphasize your poor design skills for the operations role. **The key to this approach is that while you're still acknowledging real deficiencies, you're not suggesting that you lack skills critical to succeeding in the role.** That being said, hopefully the position for which you're interviewing aligns to your strengths anyway, so you aren't signing up for a job in which you're constantly struggling or challenged.

Ideally, your confidence in your strengths generally minimizes any question someone might have about your deficiencies. If all other answers fail, try this third option:

3. Address the question with an affirmative statement that allows you to move quickly onto the next question. A good example is, "I believe I could improve upon everything I undertake. I want to be the best, and so with that goal comes the admission that I'm not perfect or an expert. I think I have a lot of strengths, but all of those traits could still be better."

If none of the above responses work, your interviewer is one tough nut to crack. Whatever you do, don't answer the deficiencies question with a version of you being a "perfectionist" or "working too hard." Recruiters and college counselors tell me this is the oldest, and worst, trick in the book, as you only appear arrogant, or evasive, by sidestepping the question.

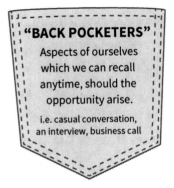

A DEFINED SKILL SET
Combination of your strengths and interests

CAPABILITY STORIES
Rehearsed 60-90 second success stories that emphasize a key strength

CAPABILITY STORIES

The second of these two "back pocketers" is carrying **several an-ecdotes that speak to your various capabilities**. What I mean by anecdotes is not what we would tell our mom or best friend. Rather, these are rehearsed 60 to 90-second stories that showcase a particular ability without sounding braggadocios. Your story could be about any number of skills you're trying to emphasize: how you're a team player, how you put the client first, how you think outside the box, how you always meet your quota, etc. Every job is different, and each one comes with a specific set of requirements and preferred qualifi-cations. Adjust your anecdotes to fit a given role.

By telling your interviewer a story that emphasizes a capability you possess — one essential to the job at hand — he or she can imagine you doing something similar for their company. Thus, your story essentially paints a picture depicting your future success. In the end, it is in a hiring manager's best interest to hire whomever they believe is the most capable candidate. Your capability stories are aiding this process forward. So, communicate your prior achievements matter-of-factly, and you allow your interviewer to look good once you are hired — and create your next capability story at their company.

Ideally, you can recall two to three of these kinds of success stories at all times. Rehearse them so they don't "sit" in your "back pocket," conjuring up dust as they await actual listeners. The tactic may seem a bit calculated, but being prepared will boost your confidence during an interview.

CHAPTER THREE

BE UNORTHODOX

"Don't compare yourself with anyone in this world...if you do so, you are insulting yourself."

- Bill Gates

BE PERSISTENT, NOT A PEST

Until now, I've cautioned you to take most advice with a healthy dose of skepticism. The experience and guidance your advisors and/or mentors provide could very well be sound advice; I hear such tidbits all the time. But just because the advice is legitimate or the person giving it is respectable, it still may be *generic* advice. And, as is the premise of this entire book, heeding average advice won't necessarily help you get a better-than-average job.

Yet, every so often, I receive an incredibly unique piece of advice that I feel compelled to store somewhere, or share with someone. I'll write the words on Post-it notes, in various notebooks, or even on my hand so I can recall it later.

One such piece of advice came from a current mentor of mine. As I mentioned in the previous chapter, after I quit my first job, I was stuck in a rut. Certain that I wanted to leave the field of journalism, I was unsure of everything else. A mutual contact introduced me to my now-mentor so I could get his thoughts on my next step. After asking this person to meet with me several times over a two-month period, he finally relented. Based on his short responses in our email communications, I assumed I was a bother. Once we met, I apologized about repeatedly reaching out to arrange the meeting. Interestingly, he complimented my follow-through, adding a somewhat surprising response: "There is a fine line between being a pest and being persistent."

While I don't think my mentor was the first to say those words, the statement has resonated with me ever since. Now, when reaching out to a new contact, I often recall his advice as I try to gauge whether I'm on the "persistent" or "pest" side of the fence.

How do we define that fence, or "fine line?" Ultimately the answer is subjective, judged by the individual with whom we're communicating. And first impressions can change. For example, if you are initially perceived as a pest in your outreach but impress your new contact in person, you may be thought of as persistent in hindsight. But if you're teetering on that pest line early in your communications, you might not be granted an in-person meeting.

Sometimes, whether someone believes you are a pest has little to do with you. When you are introduced to someone via a mutual contact, there's a lot that can happen behind the scenes. For instance, if your existing contact (your referral source) recommends you meet with someone, and that person (the referral) highly respects your mutual contact, you may not need to write an introductory email to the referral, as he or she has already set up or agreed to the meeting. This scenario is especially likely when your referral source is selective about making introductions. On the other hand, if the referral frequently receives introductions from your mutual contact, he or she might simply disregard you, or may not make it a priority to meet with you. Generally speaking, most introductions made via a mutual contact fall within the two ends of the spectrum. Unfortunately, it isn't always clear what the relationship is between the referral source and the new referral. When this relationship is unclear, you can do one or more of the following to increase your chances of getting an in-person meeting with the referral:

- Test the waters with a complimentary opening line in your initial email. Say something along the lines of "[Insert name of referral source] spoke highly of you." I utilize this tactic for two reasons:

  1. By mentioning your mutual contact upfront, he or she quickly understands your reason for emailing. This tactic is especially useful if the referral source gave your new contact a heads up that you'd be reaching out to him or her. Also, listing your mutual contact right away is often appreciated by those who prefer succinct emails.

  2. By complimenting your new contact, you've started your email—and hopefully your professional relationship—on a positive note. Also, a compliment always makes someone feel good; it doesn't really matter whether your referral source actually said something nice to you about him or her. (Such a comment is one of a select few permissible white lies).

- Research your new referral so you can include something of substance in your email that uniquely applies to the person. Most people assume an introduction made via a mutual contact will result in a meeting, so they do not take this extra step. But when I spoke to my mentor (who expressed the pest versus persistent line), he said he doesn't always respond to requests for a meeting, even when introduced through a mutual contact. When I asked him why, he provided this response: "If someone can't even differentiate themselves digitally, what makes me think they'll stand out in person? I don't want to invest my time in someone who isn't worth the time." While his words may seem insensitive, I also found them encouraging. With a little extra effort, I can immediately separate myself from others my age through a simple email. After discussing this idea with dozens of mentors and advisors, I've learned that there are generally three types of "outreach emails" that people receive:

  - **Ordinary**: The typical introductory email will include: 2-3 sentences, his or her name, where they work or what their career interest is, the name of the mutual contact, and some version of "[name of mutual contact] suggested we meet." The positive of this email approach is that it is succinct. The negative is that it isn't memorable.

  - **Noteworthy**: A less amateur approach to crafting an outreach email is mentioning one of the referral's fun facts or achievements and how you found it particularly interesting or impressive. For instance, maybe you saw that he or she is a big hockey fan, or you both graduated from the same university. Whatever the "fun fact" you include, this can typically be found via a quick online search. This type of email is thoughtful but could also be considered rudimentary, as you do not know how often he or she grants meetings with new people. If often, you won't likely be the only person ever to compliment him or her on a particularly obvious achievement. The positive of this email approach is that you are putting forth extra effort. The negative is that it isn't much effort.

- **Thoughtful**: I always assume I'm one of several people asking someone for a meeting at a given time, which forces me to craft an email that is both thoughtful and unique to the individual. Sometimes page 2 or 3 of an online search of the person can provide random nuggets. If you come up empty, what about asking your mutual contact? He or she might have a few stories or extra intel on the person. By identifying something different in your outreach email, you are inherently demonstrating that a meeting with this person would be very meaningful for you. You don't have to dig up the referral's genealogy, but illustrate that you spent a little bit of time trying to understand him or her better.

A few examples I've used in the past include someone who:

› Published a book (because I, too, wrote one)

› Lived in a city where I also once lived

› Served on the board of a familiar organization

› Had other contacts in common, beyond the initial referral source

> › Worked at a company in which I had a separate connection (e.g., I know somebody else who works there, used to work there, work(ed) in the building, etc.)

Now that we've discussed how to craft an introductory email, the cadence of your communications is just as important in getting that meeting (and avoiding the "pest" perception). While not a steadfast rule, persistence is often rewarded when following some of the below timing guidelines:

- Give him or her a week to respond to your email. You never know someone's circumstance. He or she could be launching a new project, dealing with the passing of a family member, vacationing, weeding through a clogged inbox, etc. If you haven't met, you are not yet a priority to this person. Don't expect to hear from him or her for at least a few days.

- If you do not receive a response within one week, you "should" follow up within the following week. The reason for this particular timing is because your referral might assume you are sending a similar "let's connect" email to several people simultaneously. If you take a couple weeks to follow up with this person, you are essentially sending a subtle message that a meeting with him or her would be nice, but having it won't really affect you either way. Indifference is not what you want here. Fight to be remembered and your contact will feel compelled to make the time. If you wait too long, you will probably have to re-engage your contact all over again, and that just becomes awkward. I've been there and used the "hopefully you remember me" line. Rarely do those inconsistent connections lead to fruitful relationships. Start off on the right foot, and be persistent by being consistent.

- If you feel strongly about meeting this person and you feel it is critical to your professional growth in some capacity, then send your follow-up email with no expectation of an in-person meeting. Instead, be understanding of their presumably busy work schedule, and mention that you were hoping if they weren't able to meet in person, they might have the chance to provide advice via email or over the phone. Taking this tactic demonstrates your main goal: learning from the person's experiences, rather than what job they might be able to get you. I've employed this tactic quite a bit, although it's usually because the person lives in a different state. Still, writing an email or getting someone on the phone for a few minutes is less of an investment than an in-person meeting, so this approach could be a good last resort. And who knows, maybe your persistence will be rewarded with an in-person meeting after you impress your contact over the phone!

At the end of the day, people just want to feel appreciated. If you don't appreciate someone's time or appear unappreciative in your correspondence, you will likely be put into the "pest" category.

One final thought on getting the in-person meeting: some people are just unkind. Your referral may never grant you a meeting, or provide advice, despite your efforts. So, if someone treats you as if you're being a pest, even though you've been kind and strategically patient in your communications, don't worry. At that point, you've done all you can do and this person is not worth *your time*.

GAIN "APPLYING EXPERIENCE"

The odds that your next job stems from an online posting are probably low. Still, despite this unlikelihood, thousands of jobs are posted to various websites every day... Someone has to fill them, and you might as well enter yourself into consideration.

Besides, even if you apply to a job online and nothing comes of it, there is still value in the "applying experience" you gain. By regularly applying to positions posted online, you become accustomed to expressing your skill set, qualifications, and value to a potential employer. While you might not want to regularly focus your energy on applying to a job different from the one you have (and the one that is currently paying you), it's important to understand the landscape of your industry so you can identify your approximate value in the marketplace. Applying for jobs (assuming you aren't fulfilled in your current position) a couple times a month helps you stay abreast of what is in demand in your field, including the key attributes for which employers are looking, and find valuable. Understanding these traits is helpful as you develop and grow in your career.

That said, you won't gain much "applying experience" by simply submitting a generic cover letter and résumé to every job posted online. Be selective when applying for other positions. You might think, "How can it hurt to apply to every post that seems interesting?" I would argue that it can be detrimental, as it both wastes your time and prevents you from fully focusing on your current job.

On that same note, most companies will not fill a position simply because they received someone's résumé and there happened to be a small pool of applicants. The days of nepotism and dumb luck are largely behind us, as there are too many strong candidates available today, and multiple means of contacting them. If you don't tailor your résumé to the position at hand, a hiring manager may remove you from a given pool. Because if they don't see the fit upon first glance, it's in their best interest to remove you from consideration. Remember, their jobs are on the line, too. A bad hire (i.e., someone unqualified or inexperienced) reflects poorly upon the person who made the hire. So if an applicant pool is shallow, a recruiter or employer will likely source additional candidates internally, or by re-posting the position elsewhere.

Tailoring your résumé to a specific position doesn't mean you have to start with a blank white sheet of paper. Maybe you only need to wordsmith a line or two; still, those extra five minutes can give you an advantage over the dozens of generic submissions recruiters undoubtedly receive. I have edited my résumé hundreds of times, literally. Why? Call me a perfectionist, but this one-pager represents my entire identity to someone who hasn't met me. I want to make certain that the interviewer's portrayal of me is an accurate one, and that my work experience or skills are applicable to the role.

While an updated and relevant résumé is essential for any job application, a LinkedIn profile is as important a reference to some recruiters. One can easily access your recent activity, some of your connections, and your general work experience—all via a simple on-line search. So, every time you update your résumé with new roles or responsibilities, make the same edits to your LinkedIn profile. Think of your résumé and LinkedIn profile as two sides of the same coin (with your big copper face on it): If a recruiter sees one of the two and decides to do further research, you appear thorough and organized if they mirror one another in both content and style.

While a résumé is (or "should" be) limited to a single page, the benefit of a LinkedIn profile is that you can be more elaborate. LinkedIn allows you to provide more detail on your prior experience. If you have a portfolio to link, a video to showcase, or simply need more room to write about additional responsibilities you've held, LinkedIn gives you the space. You'll want to extract the best aspects of your LinkedIn profile to compose your résumé, rather than the other way around.

Regardless of how much information you include in one location versus the other, ensure that you tell the same story. If your LinkedIn profile paints one picture of you and your résumé depicts someone entirely different, you may be unnecessarily confusing the reader. Even as you tailor your résumé to fit a specific position, your fundamental roles and responsibilities need to be the same as your LinkedIn profile.

If you are contacted for an interview after applying online, think of this opportunity as nothing more than good practice. If you find the position desirable, even better, but these conversations are merely a way for you to refine your unique message. Some people will ask if you're actively looking. If you're satisfied at your job, mention as much in your conversation. You can also add that you found the position interesting and wanted to hear more. My approach to these calls is similar to a hitter's goal in the batting cage: to shake off the rust and get reps. When you're actually in a position to move on from your employer, your applying experience will come in handy, as you've been able to distinctly craft your pitch. You'll have a better idea of what resonates with people and are likely to be less nervous when interviewing for a job you seriously want.

Maybe you are unsure of exactly what it is you want to do. Getting on the phone with a recruiter or hearing more about another job might help you narrow down a tighter career direction—or maybe not. Either way, applying online or taking a phone interview every so often doesn't take up an inordinate amount of time, so why not do so?

GO BEYOND "DOING YOUR HOMEWORK"

You've probably heard the saying, "Do your homework." To those on the job hunt, this is another way of suggesting to prepare for an up-coming job interview or do research ahead of a job application. Doing your homework is a common piece of advice, and definitely one worth taking. But why stop there? You're looking to obtain a better than average job, so you need to go beyond "doing your homework" to stand out and achieve that goal.

Let's say you've come across a job posting that sounds interesting. Did you find the post on LinkedIn? If so, does it indicate who the recruiter is? If so, click on that person's profile. Does he or she list any contact information? If not, why don't you send him or her a private message requesting their email address? Sometimes you have to request a "LinkedIn Connection" before you can send someone a message. Sure, it may seem a little unorthodox to request a connection to someone you technically don't "know" (and they might also think it's weird). But if you send a compelling message and/or email with your request, simply mentioning your desire to learn more about the position, you might hear back from the recruiter. If you receive no response, there's no harm done except for the few minutes it took to craft the message.

If you decide to take this tactic and request a connection with the recruiter, try to avoid sending a generic message. Sending a private message may be especially prudent if the position requires additional information not listed in the description. Sending an "I'd love to hear more about this job, as I think I'm a great fit" doesn't really engage the recruiter or necessarily elicit a response. If you ask genuinely relevant questions that the description doesn't sufficiently answer, you may actually be perceived as more conscientious than the remainder of applicants. Further, if you have thoroughly read the position *and* sent job materials that specifically address why you are a suitable candidate (instead of a generic résumé submission), you may be giving yourself a leg up on the competition before you've even walked in the door.

Tailoring your résumé or personally contacting a recruiter may seem like insignificant tactics that don't necessarily reap dividends, but it's the *accumulation* of these and other strategies that increases your chances of consideration. And if you're not taking these steps, small as they may seem, you will likely be just another white sheet of paper that gets lost in the shuffle.

Imagine you're a recruiter. You might be drowning in résumés and candidates vying for the position you recently posted. If one of the candidates sends you a message on LinkedIn, at the very least it will allow his or her name to stand out. Then the recruiter can explore further whether the candidate meets the requirements for the position. People are generally overworked and, more often than not, welcome opportunities to reduce their workload. This can be especially true if the recruiter has several other vacancies to fill. By reaching out to him or her, in addition to applying on the job board or company website, you are essentially putting your candidacy toward the top of the applicant list. Assuming you are qualified for the role, you might actually be doing the recruiter a favor by saving them time they would have otherwise spent interviewing candidates.

One final thought on personally contacting the recruiter: Even if you may not be a complete fit for the position, perhaps you know someone who is. If so, don't be afraid to offer that suggestion to the person hiring. He or she might be surprised at the recommendation, but also pleased that you recognized the mismatch, as well as the possibility that you could help fill the role. I've done this for a few people, and, while it has yet to come full circle for me, I know that both sides have appreciated the gesture. I consider it karma, which will eventually come to benefit me somehow, someday.

CREATE A STANDOUT RÉSUMÉ

Creating a standout résumé does not come with a set of hard-and-fast rules. Certainly, an aesthetic layout and having no grammatical errors are important criteria, but, ultimately, the content matters most. However, there are certain ways in which that content can be presented that might help your résumé stand out within the stack.

One of these ways is to use a hint of color on the page. Some people use a lot of color. Less color generally carries more impact, but the amount you use really depends on the layout. Whether you use colors to designate different sections, or highlight prior achievements via some visually appealing infographic, create something that makes you proud.

Not the most adept in graphic design? That's okay. You don't really need to be. The takeaway is to create one sheet that highlights your past accomplishments and transferable skills in an aesthetic way that stands out to recruiters, whose eyes glaze over résumés all day, every day. No matter what layout you choose, try to aim for a minimalistic approach, using one type of font throughout the page. Cleaner fonts like Calibri, Arial, Verdana, and Segoe UI are a few good examples.

Another way to get your résumé to stand out is to include a line that shows off a bit of your personality. I prefer to position this tidbit under the "Additional Skills" section, so it's not entirely out of place or random. Sometimes, this becomes a talking point in an interview, often eliciting a small laugh when someone reads my résumé in front of me. In interviews, people tend to be so serious; a fun fact can be a nice deviation. It also demonstrates that you are not solely a product of your papered achievements and you have an actual personality.

Besides tailoring the content of my résumé for various job applications, I have also played around with the layout over the years. While I finally feel as though it is now in a good place, I will probably continue to revise it as I encounter new trends or get inspiration from other résumés. Below, you can see the evolution of my résumé layout. Ultimately, my goal is to make the reader clearly grasp my candidacy by doing the following:

- Separating my contact information from the content sections (Professional Experience, Education, and Additional Skills) by using a dark blue line that takes up the width of the page. One way to do this effectively while maximizing space is to decrease the top margin and include your contact information in the "Header."

- Using one consistent color, but sparingly. I applied that same dark blue color to my section titles. I didn't want to include more than two colors (I used black for the remainder of text) so the layout didn't distract from the content.

- Decreasing the left and right margins so there is ample white space in between the sections. I wanted the sections to be clearly distinct, even if it made the page a bit tight.

- Specifically formatting the font in various ways:

  - I bolded the section titles so the reader always knows what section they are in.

  - I capitalized the full name of my employers so the reader doesn't have to search long on the page to find them.

  - I italicized each job title (and kept the text lowercase) so the roles are distinct from both the employer and the specific responsibilities I held at each position.

  - I indented the content listed in the Additional Skills section and organized them by dash marks. While my main skills could be derived from the actual positions I've held (listed under Professional Experience), I indented these additional skills to illustrate that they were utilized in one or more positions I've held during my career.

- Showcasing my personality. My "fun fact" (listed in the Additional Skills section) is that I'm a "peanut butter aficionado." I'm not entirely certain what it takes to be a "peanut butter aficionado," but I am quite knowledgeable about the condiment. Also, it seemed both harmless and a decent conversation piece. Anything you have passion for and can have a lighthearted conversation about will work as a fun fact. If you are unsure, ask your friends if there is anything "quirky" about you, and see if you can come up with a one-liner from there.

  - A few examples of others' fun facts include: avid fan of a particular sports team, hold dual citizenship, ran multiple half or full marathons, brews his own beer, etc.

MOST RECENT (2015):

WHITNEY BLAINE
EMAIL ADDRESS
MAILING   ADDRESS
CITY, STATE
CONTACT   NUMBER

Professional Experience

(MOST RECENT) COMPANY NAME, CITY, STATE
Position Held, Start Date – End Date
- Insert 3-4 sentences about the roles and responsibilities held during role, inc. major achievements/quantifiable information.
- Insert 3-4 sentences about the roles and responsibilities held during role, inc. major achievements/quantifiable information.
- Insert 3-4 sentences about the roles and responsibilities held during role, inc. major achievements/quantifiable information.
- Insert 3-4 sentences about the roles and responsibilities held during role, inc. major achievements/quantifiable information.

COMPANY "B" NAME, CITY, STATE
Position Held, Start Date – End Date
- Insert 3-4 sentences about the roles and responsibilities held during role, inc. major achievements/quantifiable information.
- Insert 3-4 sentences about the roles and responsibilities held during role, inc. major achievements/quantifiable information.
- Insert 3-4 sentences about the roles and responsibilities held during role, inc. major achievements/quantifiable information.
- Insert 3-4 sentences about the roles and responsibilities held during role, inc. major achievements/quantifiable information.

COMPANY "C" NAME, CITY, STATE
Position Held, Start Date – End Date
- Insert 3-4 sentences about the roles and responsibilities held during role, inc. major achievements/quantifiable information.
- Insert 3-4 sentences about the roles and responsibilities held during role, inc. major achievements/quantifiable information.
- Insert 3-4 sentences about the roles and responsibilities held during role, inc. major achievements/quantifiable information.
- Insert 3-4 sentences about the roles and responsibilities held during role, inc. major achievements/quantifiable information.

COMPANY "D" NAME, CITY, STATE
Position Held, Start Date – End Date
- Insert 3-4 sentences about the roles and responsibilities held during role, inc. major achievements/quantifiable information.
- Insert 3-4 sentences about the roles and responsibilities held during role, inc. major achievements/quantifiable information.
- Insert 3-4 sentences about the roles and responsibilities held during role, inc. major achievements/quantifiable information.
- Insert 3-4 sentences about the roles and responsibilities held during role, inc. major achievements/quantifiable information.

COMPANY "E" NAME, CITY, STATE
Position Held, Start Date – End Date
- Insert 3-4 sentences about the roles and responsibilities held during role, inc. major achievements/quantifiable information.
- Insert 3-4 sentences about the roles and responsibilities held during role, inc. major achievements/quantifiable information.
- Insert 3-4 sentences about the roles and responsibilities held during role, inc. major achievements/quantifiable information.
- Insert 3-4 sentences about the roles and responsibilities held during role, inc. major achievements/quantifiable information.

Education

UNIVERSITY NAME, CITY, STATE
Name of Major, Minor (if applicable), Year of Graduation
- GPA, Academic Awards received (if applicable).
- Other Awards received (if applicable).

Additional Skills

- Author of one book, editor of another
- Web Analytics (Omniture, OWA, Google Analytics)
- HTML/CSS (Dreamweaver, Wordpress)
- Sponsorship valuations and negotiations
- Nationally-ranked high school volleyball player
- Peanut butter aficionado

- Accepted into USC Annenberg Advantage Mentor Program
- Social Media Strategy (Topsy, Socialbakers, Keyy)
- Sound/Video Editing (Audacity, Avid, FinalCut, iMovie)
- Microsoft Office Suite (PPT, Excel, Word)
- Competitive runner
- Intermediate Spanish speaker

EVOLUTION (Over four years):

Whitney Blaine

Contact Number
Mailing Address
City, State Zipcode
Email Address

Journalism Experience

Collegiate
Most Recent Collegiate Involvement -- Start Date to End Date
• Insert one or two sentences that speak to the roles and responsibilities you held during role, inc. any skills developed
Second Collegiate Activity -- Start Date to End Date
• Insert one or two sentences that speak to the roles and responsibilities you held during role, inc. any skills developed
Third Collegiate Activity -- Start Date to End Date
• Insert one or two sentences that speak to the roles and responsibilities you held during role, inc. any skills developed
Fourth Collegiate Activity -- Start Date to End Date
• Insert one or two sentences that speak to the roles and responsibilities you held during role, inc. any skills developed

Professional
Company Name -- Start Date to End Date
• Insert one or two sentences that speak to the roles and responsibilities you held during role, inc. any skills developed

Internships
Most Recent Internship -- Start Date to End Date
• Insert one or two sentences that speak to the roles and responsibilities you held during role, inc. any skills developed
Second Internship/Leadership Role -- Start Date to End Date
• Insert one or two sentences that speak to the roles and responsibilities you held during role, inc. any skills developed
Third Internship/Leadership Role -- Start Date to End Date
• Insert one or two sentences that speak to the roles and responsibilities you held during role, inc. any skills developed
Fourth Internship/Leadership Role -- Start Date to End Date
• Insert one or two sentences that speak to the roles and responsibilities you held during role, inc. any skills developed

Personal

Objective
Insert one liner about job, internship or position you are looking for, including the applicable field or industry.

Education
University Name
Applicable Major -- GPA: X.X
Applicable Minor -- GPA: X.X
Graduation: Month, Year

Skills
• Skill 1 (Include applicable programs)
• Skill 2 (Include applicable programs)
• Skill 3 (Include applicable programs)
• Interest 1
• Interest 2
• Fun fact 1
• Fun Fact 2

Awards
• Award Received 1
• Award Received 2
• Award Received 3
• Award Received 4

References

Reference #1	Reference #2	Reference #3	Reference #4
Reference Title	Reference Title	Reference Title	Reference Title
Reference Employer	Reference Employer	Reference Employer	Reference Employer
Contact Number	Contact Number	Contact Number	Contact Number
Contact Email	Contact Email A	Contact Email	Contact Email

2011 — This is the earliest version of what I deem my "professional résumé" (résumés in high school don't apply). When I look back at this version, I can't help but laugh. I was trying to do so much. That's the worst thing you can do in a résumé. Try to avoid throwing in the "kitchen sink," unlike what I did here. The sections indicating "collegiate," "professional" and "internships" are confusing and out of order. Also, I ambitiously included four references - not only is that an eyesore, but it's overkill, and others will likely perceive it as such. As you will see in my résumé evolution on the following pages, I opted for the mantra "simpler is better." Sometimes you might think a nifty design will separate you, but if that design only confuses the reader, it will likely produce the opposite effect.

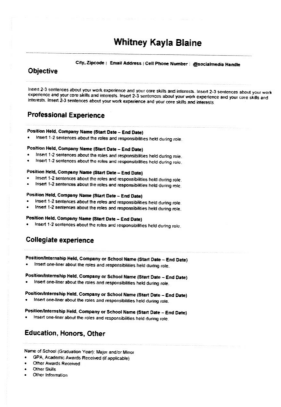

2012 — This is one of the earliest versions of my résumé. The font is distracting, and there are too many horizontal lines that take up the width of the page which distract from the text. You can't see the color here but the large horizontal line that separates my name from my contact information is bright red. A big no no, I realize years later. While this version is fine as a first pass, it doesn't allow the reader to fully grasp my unique value or achievements because there are too many embellishments and, thus, not enough "meat" substantiating why I'm a qualified hire.

Whitney Blaine
NAME OF STREET
CITY, STATE
CELL PHONE NUMBER
EMAIL ADDRESS

Summary and Objective

Insert 2-3 sentences about your work experience and your core skills and interests. Insert 2-3 sentences about your work experience and your core skills and interests. Insert 2-3 sentences about your work experience and your core skills and interests. Insert 2-3 sentences about your work experience and your core skills and interests.

Professional Experience

COMPANY A, CITY, STATE
Position Held, Start Date – End Date
- Insert 1-2 sentences about the roles and responsibilities held during role.
- Insert 1-2 sentences about the roles and responsibilities held during role.

COMPANY B, CITY, STATE
Position Held, Start Date – End Date
- Insert 1-2 sentences about the roles and responsibilities held during role.
- Insert 1-2 sentences about the roles and responsibilities held during role.

COMPANY C, CITY, STATE
Position Held, Start Date – End Date
- Insert 1-2 sentences about the roles and responsibilities held during role.
- Insert 1-2 sentences about the roles and responsibilities held during role.

COMPANY D, CITY, STATE
Position Held, Start Date – End Date
- Insert 1-2 sentences about the roles and responsibilities held during role.
- Insert 1-2 sentences about the roles and responsibilities held during role.

COMPANY E, CITY, STATE
Position Held, Start Date – End Date
- Insert 1-2 sentences about the roles and responsibilities held during role.
- Insert 1-2 sentences about the roles and responsibilities held during role.

Education

COLLEGE, CITY, STATE
Name of Major, Month and Year of Graduation Date
- GPA, Academic Awards received (if applicable), minor received (if applicable).
- Other Awards received.

Additional Skills

- Video Editing (Avid, FinalCut Pro, iMovie)
- HTML/CSS (Dreamweaver)
- Sound Editing (Audacity)
- Photo Editing (Photoshop Adobe Suite, Microsoft Office)
- Social Media Strategy (Tracky, SocialGrade, etc.)
- Web Analytics (Omniture, Google Analytics, OWA)

2013 — I changed the color scheme from the red/ black to navy/black. You can't see the color here but a dark blue is used for each section heading. I employed this tactic because it served a dual purpose: it was a nice differentiator from the black text, while also acting as a section separator. Also, notice how this version and my résumé from 2012 includes a summary/objective section at the top of the page? These days, a good cover letter should replace this item.

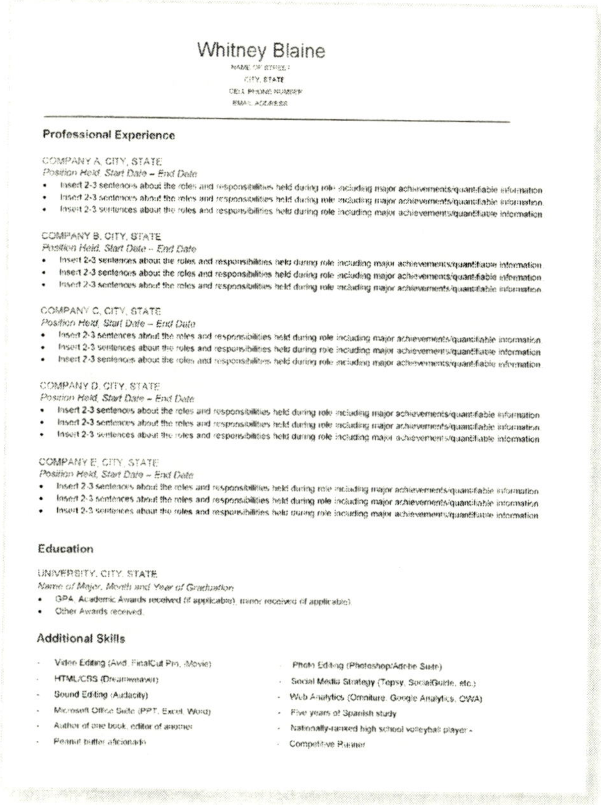

Whitney Blaine

NAME OF STREET

CITY, STATE

CELL PHONE NUMBER

EMAIL ADDRESS

Professional Experience

COMPANY A, CITY, STATE

Position Held, Start Date – End Date

- Insert 2-3 sentences about the roles and responsibilities held during role including major achievements/quantifiable information
- Insert 2-3 sentences about the roles and responsibilities held during role including major achievements/quantifiable information
- Insert 2-3 sentences about the roles and responsibilities held during role including major achievements/quantifiable information

COMPANY B, CITY, STATE

Position Held, Start Date – End Date

- Insert 2-3 sentences about the roles and responsibilities held during role including major achievements/quantifiable information
- Insert 2-3 sentences about the roles and responsibilities held during role including major achievements/quantifiable information
- Insert 2-3 sentences about the roles and responsibilities held during role including major achievements/quantifiable information

COMPANY C, CITY, STATE

Position Held, Start Date – End Date

- Insert 2-3 sentences about the roles and responsibilities held during role including major achievements/quantifiable information
- Insert 2-3 sentences about the roles and responsibilities held during role including major achievements/quantifiable information
- Insert 2-3 sentences about the roles and responsibilities held during role including major achievements/quantifiable information

COMPANY D, CITY, STATE

Position Held, Start Date – End Date

- Insert 2-3 sentences about the roles and responsibilities held during role including major achievements/quantifiable information
- Insert 2-3 sentences about the roles and responsibilities held during role including major achievements/quantifiable information
- Insert 2-3 sentences about the roles and responsibilities held during role including major achievements/quantifiable information

COMPANY E, CITY, STATE

Position Held, Start Date – End Date

- Insert 2-3 sentences about the roles and responsibilities held during role including major achievements/quantifiable information
- Insert 2-3 sentences about the roles and responsibilities held during role including major achievements/quantifiable information
- Insert 2-3 sentences about the roles and responsibilities held during role including major achievements/quantifiable information

Education

UNIVERSITY, CITY, STATE

Name of Major, Month and Year of Graduation

- GPA, Academic Awards received (if applicable), Honor received (if applicable)
- Other Awards received

Additional Skills

- Video Editing (Avid, FinalCut Pro, iMovie)
- HTML/CSS (Dreamweaver)
- Sound Editing (Audacity)
- Microsoft Office Suite (PPT, Excel, Word)
- Author of one book, editor of another
- Peanut butter aficionado
- Photo Editing (Photoshop/Adobe Suite)
- Social Media Strategy (Topsy, SocialGuide, etc.)
- Web Analytics (Omniture, Google Analytics, OWA)
- Five years of Spanish study
- Nationally-ranked high school volleyball player -
- Competitive Runner

2014 — Compared to earlier versions, this version is much closer to what my résumé looks like today. The layout is tighter, the use of color is more deliberate, and the summary/objective section has been removed to make room for more content. Overall, this version is completely passable, but you'll notice the latest version has a punchier look, utilizing a cleaner font and smaller margins (which makes it feel more robust).

REFERENCES AVAILABLE UP FRONT,
NOT "UPON REQUEST"

The average résumé commonly includes the phrase "References Available Upon Request." If you're applying to a job, how do these four words improve your résumé and, consequently, your perceived value? Knowing space is limited, every single line on your one-page résumé ought to be purposeful. The majority of good jobs stem from referrals, or people within our immediate circles, thus creating little use for this line; it's an unnecessary addition and outdated tactic. Even when applying to a job online, there's no need to indicate that you'll provide a reference at a later point. What if a hiring manager is in a rush to filter candidates to the next round and needs to know immediately whether you're a worthy candidate?

As the job market continues to become more competitive, you have to seek out any **point of differentiation**. Instead of passively stamping those four words onto the bottom of your résumé—waiting to provide actual references until they're requested—you can be proactive and provide them with a reference in advance. You can list your references in the body of an introductory email, in your cover letter, or within your actual résumé. Out of room? Replace the tried "References Available Upon Request" line, creating a 1 row by 4 column table, filling each cell with the name and phone number of two relevant sources. It's quick, easy to do, effective and one small way to separate yourself.

Ultimately, an *actual* letter of recommendation will be the most impressive to a prospective employer, especially if provided up front, at
the same time as your résumé. You could wait to send the letters (aim
for obtaining 2–3) until after you've met with the interviewer or hiring
manager, but sometimes providing references in tandem with your
résumé indicates that you're buttoned up and organized, in addition
to being a solid candidate (assuming your letters say as much). Also,
the interviewer can always choose not to read them. Why not give
them the option?

A tangible (or digital) reference letter circumvents the traditional
system. Unless you're applying to college, or a new job, you might
not have previously considered the need for a papered recommendation. Now, a word-of-mouth reference will always be helpful, as it
can open doors you didn't know existed. But a tangible letter of recommendation is sometimes equally, if not more, valuable in obtaining a job, as you're providing documentation for your work product
and character – written by someone who has seen you firsthand.

Also, a letter of recommendation often replaces a physical call to a
reference. While all your references will include his/her contact information, there is a slim chance that a recruiter actually calls the
reference after reading their letter. That's not to say the recruiter or
hiring manager won't put in a call, but that also assumes they will be
incredibly thorough. If your in-person interview supports the papered
references, you essentially save the recruiter time he or she would otherwise spend playing phone tag with your references, who may or may
not be the person to answer the phone (i.e., if he or she provides an office number). More importantly, letters of recommendation often paint

the best possible picture of you. You've seen your reference letters; they are presumably flattering and extremely positive. Because your reference took his or her time, they were likely proofread. You don't know whether your reference will paint the same picture if contacted via phone, when in the midst of a work day, if they are rushed, etc.

Of course you'll want your letters to be written by people who can sufficiently speak to your work experience and product. Former or current colleagues/bosses will always be your best source. For advice on asking a colleague to write you a letter of recommendation, see chapter 6.

If possible, have your reference sign their letter and then save it into a .pdf or uneditable format. By doing this, you are essentially saying to the hiring manager, "Yes, I have read this letter of recommendation, and it speaks very highly of me; however, it is authentic, and I did not make any changes to this person's words." It is common for people to write their own letters of recommendation and have their reference sign off on it; if you can, avoid that practice. You want a letter to give a glowing recommendation, but you don't want it to be fawning. It's pretty difficult to be objective about yourself. Also, reading someone else's words gives you better insight into how people perceive you. Just be sure to give someone a proper amount of lead time to write the letter!

An ideal letter of recommendation is both vague and specific. If you can, suggest to your recommender to speak about your strengths more generally. You'll want the language in the letter to work for a variety of job applications, including different roles and levels. Also, if the letter is strong enough, you may want to use it again a few years down the road. Hopefully it is broad enough, focusing more on your skill set and how you're a valuable employee more than on any one project or assignment you've completed.

DISREGARD THE TRADITIONAL DEFINITION OF "NETWORKING"

Our means for connecting and methods of communicating evolve every day; as such, the way we've traditionally defined "networking" is now obsolete. The mixers and conferences our dads or moms commonly attend may be fruitful for initial connections and learning opportunities, such as emerging trends in an industry or hearing from reputable industry leaders. These days, however, the bring-your-business-cards-in-bulk networking events rarely result in the creation of authentic and long-lasting professional relationships.

Some companies today even discourage their employees from using business cards. While the majority of organizations still print them, the thought behind business cards is outdated: Millennials tend to focus on the number of people we can get in front of, to whom we can hand our card, as opposed to the quality of relationships we can foster.

Along with the term "networking," "mixer" is another word we ought to rethink. Say your goal is to develop contacts in a particular industry, so you attend a relevant mixer that can help you meet more people. What makes an event like this inherently difficult is our brain's capacity to remember multiple names and faces at one time, including any stories or facts associated to each individual. Several studies have indicated that our visual memory has a finite storage capacity, generally falling within a range of 3–5 items at any given time.[5] Knowing this limitation, what does "mixing" around a large room making several quick, superficial

[5] www.pnas.org/content/105/16/5975.full#sec-5

connections do for you? If you remember only half the facts, or worse, call someone by the wrong name, those mistakes are sure to hold you back more than anything else you could have said or done.

The previous notion of "networking" needs to be redefined. As it exists today, it's too overwhelming and not at all realistic. Rather than transactionally handing out business cards like a blackjack dealer, be selective about the number of people you talk to at any given function. If we approach these types of events (e.g., workshops, panels, conferences, etc.) as an avenue for building *meaningful*, one-on-one connections, then we can actually reap the full benefits of these functions. Otherwise we're fooling ourselves into thinking we maximized our opportunity simply by showing up, but in reality we're only moving in place.

"Mutually beneficial partnerships, like any relationship, take time, patience, and mutual effort."

For lack of a better term, I'll call this tactic "coupling" (although Gwyneth Paltrow recently coined this term to mean something entirely different, so please do not associate this word with any romantic connotation). Ideally, "coupling" works best when you engage in just two to three truly interesting conversations at a single event. While at an event, you're bound to run into someone who conceives of "networking" in the traditional sense. This person will likely greet you quickly, providing you just a few minutes of their time as he or she tries to identify how you can help them. Let these people go, as it's not in your best interest to amass professional connections like a drive-thru! Mutually beneficial partnerships, like any relationship, take time, patience, and mutual effort.

Once at the event, you might wonder how to single out individuals and approach them for conversation (i.e., begin "coupling"). Quite honestly, it can be difficult. Our senses are usually so overstimulated at these sort of events—from your disappointment at the subpar buffet you waited all day to eat; to perusing the event's hectic itinerary; to navigating the sea of people in line for drinks; to simply knowing where to go next—there is no right and wrong tactic. Functions differ in size and scope, so I'll speak generally about my experience. When I first arrive at a networking event, there are two instinctive steps I take: I leave expectations at the door, and I survey the room.

- **Leave expectations at the door:** Attending an event without the presumption of meeting someone specific or the expectation of a particular conversation, you are thereby opening yourself up to new opportunities. While it is fine to go into an event with a designated goal in mind (e.g., speak to one of the panelists and let them know about your business idea), allow yourself enough flexibility that your night doesn't become a total waste if you didn't accomplish this goal. Another reason to remove all expectation is because your determination can be visible to others, and paradoxically, prevent your end goal. For instance, if you come into an event with the hope of distributing at least 10 business cards, you may rub someone the wrong way if you aggressively provide a card too early into the conversation.

We all know those people, and they are often seen "schmoozing" with multiple people rather than taking a sincere interest in one or two individuals. Also, even if you successfully hand out all 10 cards, how much time are you realistically going to spend with each person? A rushed conversation can signify insincerity.

- **Survey the room.** By "survey" I don't mean to imply that I'm judging those in attendance (although I'm sure I subconsciously do that, too). When I survey a room, I look around hoping to spot a familiar face. If I'm unsuccessful, I at least try to find a friendly face. If I don't stumble upon either a familiar or friendly face, then I just muster up whatever charisma I can, introduce myself to someone, and express interest in him or her by asking open-ended questions: How did you hear about the event? What brings you here? What field are you in/company do you work for?

"Coupling" isn't a perfect science, but as long as you maintain your authenticity, you will eventually foster meaningful relationships. Even if a contact ends up being a dead end (i.e., they didn't exchange contact information with you, walked away in the middle of your conversation, or never responded to your "nice meeting you" email post-event), don't get frustrated. Some people will continue to "network" the way they always have. We can't worry about them. As you devote more time to a lot less people, you will notice your relationships become more fulfilling. When we focus less on our own interests and more on learning about and helping a particular individual, we develop deeper connections.

An advisor of mine also felt that traditional networking was antiquated. She provided me with the following advice, which has proved to be a pivotal truth throughout my career: The best connections are already accessible; just look within your immediate circle of contacts to find them. At the next networking event you attend, see if you can forge a relationship by playing the name game (i.e., determining whether he or she knows any of the same people as you). Sharing contacts or swapping stories is crucial to forging a relationship. Just as you might look for a "similar circumstance" in an introductory email to a new contact, finding a common bond also strengthens in-person conversations. By sharing a mutual contact—even if you don't know the third party that well—you're establishing roots that are critical to the development of a worthwhile business connection.

A word of caution with this approach: Your mutual contact might be someone you both dislike. For whatever reason, if your shared contact is believed to be a universal jackass, then you might want to have a laugh over that person's ridiculous behavior. It's easy to get into this habit, and before you know it, you're speaking negatively about someone *with someone* you barely know. Stories can get misconstrued all the time, and you may end up looking petty if the anecdote is ever recounted. Don't fall into this trap if you can help it. If someone baits you into badmouthing another, speak in generalities, such as "yeah [insert name] is definitely an interesting person." Then quickly change subjects or suggest another potential mutual contact. Hopefully, the person you're speaking with will sense that you don't want to bond with them by insulting another. That said, you can apply this suggestion to any discussion you have with someone about someone else. Don't utter a bad word about anyone, even if your contact doesn't know the other person. It's too difficult to decipher whether someone is trustworthy upon an initial meeting.

For those looking to connect with others *outside* of their given industry, "coupling" might not be the best tactic. For example, let's say
you decide to start a company but need developers to build out the
technology. You don't currently know any engineers, so you attend a
relevant technology conference, both for the knowledge you can gain
and the opportunity to meet skilled engineers. Ultimately your goal
in attending this event is the same as the one described earlier: *spend
the majority of your time with an individual, rather than the collective.*
While it's not a bad idea to have a stack of business cards handy for
anyone willing to listen to you, see if you can forge a bond with one
person ingrained in this other industry. Ideally this person will serve as
your "gatekeeper" for the duration of the event. This person is essentially your professional wingman: he or she (usually gregarious and a
center of influence) can steer you in the right direction, or introduce
you to colleagues who might be interested in your business plan. But
be upfront about your objective or offer up some enticing incentive for
the gatekeeper so he or she doesn't feel as if you are taking advantage.
If the gatekeeper needs to leave early or has other business to tend to,
ask him or her for suggestions on any other relevant conferences or
events. See if he or she can help you get into these other events, especially if the guest list is limited to established professionals in the field.

Perhaps your sole reason for attending a networking event is because
you are considering a career change but don't know anybody in the
field. If this sounds like you, then reverting to the traditional notion of
"networking" (e.g., distributing mass business cards, sending indis-
criminate follow-up emails, etc.) might have to be your starting point.
Getting hired into an entirely new industry is a daunting task, as you'll
most likely have to build a completely new network. Networking events

are helpful in meeting new people, even if not knowing anyone feels initially awkward. If you are open to learning and present yourself as an already competent and experienced person (just in a different field), others may be open to helping you. Ultimately, you'll never know whether someone can help you until you attend an event. For further tips on navigating a career change, see chapter 5.

TALK TO STRANGERS

Growing up, our parents told us not to talk to strangers. And that practice was warranted at a young age—it was meant for our safety. Fast forward to our adult life, and the same rule doesn't apply. We don't need to be cloaked in protection today like we once were. Now is the time to interact with those strangers—and to connect with them.

"The practice of talking to strangers can literally be applied anywhere, anytime."

The practice of talking to strangers can literally be applied anywhere, anytime. If you meet someone on a plane or while on vacation in another country, for instance, your communication doesn't have to end after that initial encounter. We live in a world of readily accessible information. Your paths can cross again whenever both parties choose to reconnect.

Keeping an open mind is key to effectively talk with strangers. We all have times when we're tired or don't feel like socializing. Sometimes, however, the most random conversations end up as the most fruitful, and the best ideas occur in the least likely of places. If we keep an open mind to meeting new people—even when our mind or bodies are rejecting this idea—we might be setting ourselves up for future opportunities that we could not have foreseen. And while it may be difficult to assess the value of a 15-minute discussion with someone while waiting in line at jury duty, you simply don't know what can happen if you don't at least try.

As you keep an open mind, throw all judgment out the window. Talking to strangers is most effective—and rewarding—when you aren't selective about whom you engage. Interesting people come from all kinds of backgrounds, ages, and experiences. We can learn something from anybody, no matter his or her circumstance. If a business connection doesn't result from your brief encounter, your conversation was not useless; you become more courageous with every stranger you approach.

A fairly obvious word of caution when talking to strangers: let your intuition be your guide. If someone doesn't exude a decent vibe, he or she is probably not worth the outreach or effort. Sometimes we'll meet an individual who appears established and/or successful, and we want them to be a great person, but something simply feels amiss. Your gut will always be your best advisor. Be as nice as possible to the person, but as soon *as possible*, try to find the most polite exit. There are plenty of good-natured and successful people in the world; you don't need to waste any energy on those who have bad intentions.

Here's an example of how talking to a stranger resulted in me meeting one of my greatest mentors to date. At 22 years old, I was a reporter covering college football. When USC played Notre Dame that year, I flew from LA to Chicago, and then rented a car to South Bend, Indiana. Between the travel to the game, my early flight the following day, and the work I needed to submit, I slept about three hours in a little over two days. Thankfully, I got an aisle seat on the plane. But as I lay back in my seat in the hopes of getting some shuteye, a nice man in the middle seat next to me started talking. He noticed my camera, and mentioned that he and his son also attended the game. He was in his late 40s/early 50s and had a generally nice aura. He didn't seem like he needed to impress anybody. He talked about his wife, kids, about how exciting the game was—random small talk.

I soon learned that he worked in private equity. Of course, I wondered why he was in a coach seat (sitting in the middle no less), but I didn't think it was a fair question to ask. And honestly, I was more concerned with my lack of sleep than judging his seating preference. But the more we talked, the more I learned about his business and the world in which he worked, something I knew little about. While I had no idea I would still get advice from him even to this day, I learned the importance of quickly conducting myself and maintaining my professionalism. Since then, I rarely turn down the opportunity to have a new conversation. In addition to the life lesson I learned, I also gained a great business connection.

Hopefully, this example also illustrates that talking to strangers in different industries is as useful as talking to people with whom you have a lot in common. Limiting our interactions to those within our own industries minimizes our opportunities. Again, I emphasize keeping an open mind. Sectors collide all the time. New ideas can arise anywhere. And, at the very least, we can always learn from someone else.

Maybe you want to amass connections with people of varying industries and backgrounds, but you aren't sure *how* to form those relationships. Unfortunately, finding a common bond with a total stranger requires several things to align simultaneously, including mutual effort and good timing, among other intangibles. What works with one individual isn't necessarily going to resonate the same way with someone else. In general, if your goal is to strengthen or expand your network, talking to strangers is a great means to this end. Here are a couple tactics that may help you foster new connections:

- First, adjust your approach to fit the individual. Just as you wouldn't greet every friend the same, adjust your tone and conversation to the contact. This statement may seem contradictory to my earlier point about not judging a stranger. It isn't, as the previous point assumed you would judge an individual and prevent a conversation from happening. Here I am suggesting to engage and converse with the individual, while making snap judgments that allow you to navigate the conversation and increase the quality of your discussion.

- Second, think about what social currency you can offer someone. Information itself is valuable, so sharing something interesting might increase your odds of stimulating a dialogue. For instance, let's say you have an interest in technology and recently heard about a new invention that affects a wide variety of people. If you found this invention or information interesting, perhaps the stranger next to you will also. So why not bring it up? It could seem entirely random to the person, but it could also be a good bridge to begin a less-random conversation. If you need a reason for what made you bring up such news, perhaps mention that something you just read caused you to think of it. Fiction books are also a great conversation piece, as they are generic and not too personal or controversial. Talk about a popular book that you've recently read, and speak to why you found it interesting. Encourage him or her to pick up a copy (I hear *Stop Doing What You Should* is a great read!).

What happens if there isn't a natural progression from your initial conversation topic? Where do you go from there? Are you struggling to find a common bond? Are you in an awkward situation (e.g., boarding a plane, in line for the restroom, etc.) that isn't ideal for a more in-depth discussion?

Maybe you don't necessarily know why you are even engaging this particular stranger, but your gut tells you they have a good sense about them, and could potentially be a worthwhile contact. If you're at that point—where it is difficult to move past the initial exchange but feel compelled to know the person further—be bold and kindly introduce yourself. Handing out a business card is also a suitable next step, especially if one of you has to leave. However, if there is time to develop the relationship further, hold off on the business card and continue looking for clues into this person's personality or background, such as the kind of bag he or she is wearing or what that person was doing before you started the conversation.

One final "maybe" to discuss in this section: Maybe the idea of talking to strangers sounds appealing, but you're afraid to be the first to initiate. If so, examine the reason(s) for your fear: Are you worried the person won't respond after you engage him? Or, if he responds curtly, are you uncertain whether to extend or end the conversation? Maybe you're concerned that he will think you're weird for randomly approaching him. Or maybe he thinks you are flirting with him.

All of those fears are legitimate and could happen when you approach a stranger. What then? Aside from a brief judgment, odd look, or uncomfortable silence, you have nothing to lose! The likelihood that something more detrimental ensues from your outreach is simply not likely. And even if you receive a weird look or awkward eye roll, so what? Except for a temporary hit to your ego, your life goes unchanged, and moments later you can move on from that person and experience.

I've been talking to strangers for what feels like my entire life (sorry, Mom!) and I've found that people will generally engage in conversation when someone expresses passion about something. Think about some of the more memorable conversations you've ever had. I bet they were interesting and collaborative, where one or both of you were extremely excited about a particular topic. Interacting with passionate and friendly people—sometimes regardless of the subject matter—is rejuvenating. Stimulating dialogue serves as a reprieve from the monotony of our daily lives. As we get lost in the stimuli of our cell phones or caught up on our next scheduled appointment, there's a uniquely gratifying quality to having a spontaneous conversation. You'll never know what could result from a simple introduction if you don't take the initiative. So go ahead and introduce yourself to the world out there. If you can't remember any of the tactics described above, a simple "hello" will suffice.

While the most obvious benefit of approaching and talking to strangers is the connections you can foster, there is also great value in the conversations themselves. People commonly say the process is often more rewarding than the product, which applies well to this theory of talking to strangers. It can be difficult regularly maintaining relationships, but the knowledge gained from your conversations could be invaluable. For every conversation I've had, I've probably only talked to 60-70 percent of those strangers a second time. Still, that yield won't reduce how often I reach out to new people, because I am guaranteed to learn something new every time.

Whether you're afraid, an "introvert," or just generally nervous about the concept of approaching new people wherever you go, there are just three things to remember:

1.   If you are cautiously optimistic, fruitful conversations and new relationships can develop anywhere.

2.   If you are open to learning, and exude passion, people will generally be warm and receptive to you.

3.   If someone isn't receptive to your outreach, there is no harm done aside from a temporary hit to your ego. Simply try again with another stranger!

DON'T FOLLOW STANDARD TIMELINES

After an initial conversation, meeting, or interview, it is customary to send the other person a thank you note. This tactic is hardly unorthodox. Actually, thank you notes are critical to the relationship-building process, so it's a step nearly everyone takes. Yet rarely do people think about the appropriate time in which to write this kind of note/email.

Being strategic about when you send your note is another way to stand out from your peers. So before you send your next thank you email, reflect on the other person's schedule: Does he or she work weekdays or weekends? Do you correspond mainly via email, or some other means? Most people think they've done their due diligence as soon as that "send" button is clicked, as the timestamp of an email might seem fairly insignificant. But if you are strategic about the time of deployment, your email has a greater chance to:

a.   Be thoroughly read

b.   Receive a response

c.   Receive a response that doesn't seem rushed

d.   Not get lost in a sea of other emails

Typically, my thank you notes are sent during one of the following three timestamps:

Friday early afternoon. If I've met with someone on or after a Wednesday in a given week, I'll send my thank you or "great to meet you" email on the subsequent Friday. Fridays typically elicit better moods, as most people have fewer emails to read or work to complete, and look forward to their weekends. Also, most people are generally more responsive at this time. However, the responses might be short and succinct, as people tend to work less on Fridays than midweek.[6]

Saturday early evening. Sending professional emails on a weekend can work to your advantage for a couple of reasons: First, by sending your message on a Saturday, you're indirectly sending another message to your contact, indicating that your prior meeting still lingered on your mind. And on the weekend no less! In this instance, most people would put the email off to Monday. But no, you want to be sure your contact knows you appreciated his/her time, and the content of your meeting was significant enough to be thought of in the midst of your weekend. Second, an email sent on the weekend is more likely to be read—even if your contact doesn't get to the email until the next morning, or that coming Monday (although most people check email every day). While this may decrease your chances of receiving a response, given that people generally disregard non-essential work emails on the weekend, the opposite might also be true. You could receive a more thoughtful response if your contact finds him or herself with more free time on the weekend.

Think about your email inbox in the middle of the workweek. Navigating that endless stream of emails is like a wave you're trying to swim in front of just enough to avoid drowning. That said, if you do send an email on a Saturday, be short and succinct. Thank the person in no more than 4–5 lines so they read it, think about you, and then respond when they get a chance. When I receive these emails, even if I don't instantly respond to someone, I am more likely

---

[6] www.getflow.com/blog/2014/07/fridays-least-productive-day-of-week/

to remember to respond at a later point, because the person's email stood out on its own, as opposed to one of a hundred I might receive on a Wednesday.

That night. Very rarely do I send a thank you note to a contact on the same day in which I've met with them. There's a reason most people have a day or two buffer; allowing time between your meeting and thank you note allows you to pop back onto your contact's radar. However, the "that night" timestamp can be useful in rare instances. Whether you felt inspired from the conversation or wanted to indicate urgency (e.g., for a desired position, the person is leaving for vacation, etc.), this kind of thank you note has to be prescriptive: project a tone that is flattering without fawning, eager but not desperate. I've probably sent 10 emails the same day in which I've met with someone—out of the thousand or so that I've sent throughout my life. The past two times were for a job I was determined to get and after an incredibly transparent and impassioned conversation.

From my conversations with millennials, it appears that many people commonly send thank you emails that same night. If you take this tactic *and* your conversation was ordinary or the meeting not very thought-provoking, utilizing this timestamp may actually hinder the development of your business relationship. Your entire correspondence—from introduction to follow up—happens in less than 24 hours. How are you supposed to foster a connection if you might not be remembered the very next day? Also, at least pretend that you have other things to do. Similar to waiting to message a date until a day or two after your initial dinner, allow your correspondence to breathe after an initial meeting.

Regardless of the timestamp you choose, be strategic about the timing of your note. You are more likely to be remembered when emailing at an uncommon time. To re-emphasize an earlier point, a timestamp outside the standard "Monday–Friday, 9am–5pm" subtly indicates that *your* working hours aren't "standard." If you emphasized your work ethic and drive in your in-person meeting, then your unusually-timed email serves as a small example of your personality and work ethic.

HAVE FREE TIME? CHECK-IN WITH PEOPLE

Find yourself with 10 minutes to spare while you wait for your lunch appointment to arrive? Use that free time to check in with people. Prioritize developing important relationships by checking in with valued contacts at least 2–3 times a year. This tactic is critical to staying on someone's radar. If you and your contact's paths don't cross much, a simple check-in on his or her birthday, over the holidays, or otherwise allows you to stay relevant.

What these check-ins are not meant to be are something that screams "what can you do for me lately?" Look at these emails as an element in fostering a relationship. They are most effective when usually short, succinct, and informal. For instance, if the football season is about to begin and a contact of mine is a passionate fan, I might send a quick email asking what he expects from his team this year.

The takeaway is not to expect anything to result from checking in with someone. Quite honestly, I don't send these emails as often as I'd like, because sometimes it seems altogether too random. But if you have a relevant tie that made you think of a contact (i.e., you passed the restaurant where you met for breakfast a year or so ago), that's as good a cause as any for checking in. People generally appreciate being thought of, and sending a check-in without any real purpose indicates you care about this person and your relationship. It also helps you become top of mind, especially if your last email exchange has been collecting dust.

If you have a terrible memory or simply can't keep track of when you last reached out to a contact, you could try to download an application or software that reminds you. There are dozens of companies out there, but one I personally use is an application for Gmail called Boomerang. With Boomerang, you can schedule an email to come back to the top of your inbox at a particular time (i.e., three months later). Microsoft Outlook app also has a feature where you can schedule your emails to send at a later date.

DON'T BE AFRAID TO MAKE A CHANGE

At some point in our lives, we'll question our professional paths. It may be only for a brief moment, but some of us will seriously doubt our path, and whether or not it will lead to our happiness. No matter where you're at in your career, you've likely already made some critical decisions to get to this point, such as your choice of major in college, what city to live in, or what career to explore.

Unfortunately, most of your decisions can no longer be altered. Undoing these decisions, such as where you attended college, isn't possible. They've been made, and they're now a part of your "past." You live where you live and work where you work because the road you took led you there. But your future path doesn't have to be predicated on your past. You are not stuck in the now because of what happened before today, because your past is just one part of your overall journey. You take new steps every day that help you lay the foundation for your future. If you're not thrilled with your current place (or pace), stop traveling along this particular road, which is only pointing toward monotony or unhappiness. Take an alternate route. Make a change for change's sake.

"You are not stuck in the now because of what happened before today, because your past is just one part of your overall journey."

Diverging from the known can be terrifying. But how else will you know what could possibly make you happier unless you make a change? The reason you're deviating from your past could be entirely random, and make no sense to anyone but you. People might question why you put forth such time and effort if only to later focus your energy elsewhere. Their doubts may even cause you to doubt. But you must remember that nobody else lives your life. Nobody else is in charge of your happiness but you, as you are the sole bearer of your life's consequences. So make a change, even if it's just for change's sake.

BE UNORTHODOX

HAVE FREE TIME?
CHECK IN WITH PEOPLE

BE PERSISTENT,
NOT A PEST

DON'T FOLLOW
STANDARD TIMELINES

GAIN
"APPLYING EXPERIENCE"

CREATE A
STANDOUT RÉSUMÉ

TALK TO
STRANGERS

DON'T BE AFRAID
TO MAKE A CHANGE

THROW AWAY YOUR TRADITIONAL
IDEA OF "NETWORKING"

CHAPTER FOUR

EXCEL AT LISTENING

*"Most of the successful people I've known
are the ones who do more listening than talking."*

- Bernard Baruch

I **KNOW MANY PEOPLE** who admit to having a limited attention span; I am sometimes guilty of being this person. Those who are easily distracted or have a lot on their plates may find it difficult to have a lengthy conversation. They fail to see the point, or find an hour-long lunch with a new contact inefficient in the midst of all their "real work." Ironically, I have found that those who often engage in these kinds of discussions tend to be the most successful. Because these people make the time to meet, and do so frequently, they become expert listeners over time. No matter your field or job, being a skilled listener enables new business opportunities, introduces meaningful relationships, and equips you with enriching stories.

I believe the most important skill to succeed in business and life is the ability to listen, predominantly because lacking this skill is so egregious. There is simply no constructive way to spin being a poor

listener. A bad listener is akin to waving a red flag to a potential employer or reference because people generally assume poor listeners are
one or more of the following:

- Waiting for their turn to speak

- Likely to interrupt others at any opportunity

- Only care about what they have to say

- Disrespectful of other people's time

Young adults are generally labeled the worst of all "bad listeners"
because we've grown up in the age of distractions. So how do we prove
them wrong? First, you have to acknowledge whether they are wrong.
Are you a bad listener? If you find yourself getting hints from others to
listen more, then chances are this is an area of development for you.
If you are actively working to become a better listener, there is a silver
lining: you are not alone. A majority of people also need to develop this
skill. But most don't have the wherewithal, or they won't admit they
need to improve in this area. By being both aware of your need to
improve *and* being willing to do so, you're already differentiating
yourself from your peers.

MAKE UP FOR YOUR INEXPERIENCE

Becoming a better listener is not that hard. It just takes reframing
your approach to conversations. If you actively listen to others as a
way to make up for your inexperience, you might be more willing to
absorb the other person's every word. By listening to and storing other

peoples' experiences, you are essentially filling in the gaps of your own inexperience. If you can imagine yourself in the speaker's shoes—grasping the relevant details, emotions, and conflict resolution—you're essentially gifting yourself with life experience *without having actually done anything but listen.* If you have older siblings, this idea of learning from the experiences of others is probably not new. If you're the youngest in your family, for instance, your go-to tactic growing up may have been to apply the opposite approach taken by your brother or sister, to see if that resonated better with your parents.

But perhaps you've never thought of applying this learn-from-others'-experience approach to your professional career. If you want to prove your worth to a potential employer and need to illustrate your experience, you'll need examples to call upon. If you don't have them at ready recall, get outside and start talking to other people about *their* experiences. The goal is not to replicate these stories in interviews or meetings. Rather, use them as figurative examples or hypothetical anecdotes that illustrate your thinking and how you would handle a given situation.

STRATEGIC LISTENING

From my brief stint as a reporter, I learned one specific listening skill that compels people to want to share things with you. It's a skill anyone can learn but not everyone can truly refine without practice. I call it "strategic listening."

Strategic listening is essentially the practice of listening to someone speak while mining for conversational nuggets that enhance your "experience portfolio." These nuggets are at the crux of your newly learned experience. If your contact illustrates an unusual scenario, or valuable skill they've utilized, pepper their story with questions so you acquire all the surrounding details that led to this person's decision or action. Obtain enough information so you can picture yourself in a similar setting.

I'm fairly overt when strategically listening. I simply express my interest in how the storyteller handled a given scenario, letting him or her know that listening to the experiences of others is how I learn best. If I feel comfortable with the person, I'll engage further, asking whether he or she might take the same action twice if provided the opportunity. Their answer usually dictates how I would handle a similar situation, as I can extract key mistakes or successes. Thus, I've learned enough details from start to finish to essentially own someone else's experience.

For example, let's say you have yet to manage a project that involved multiple people. Maybe you've been assigned more junior level responsibilities, so that opportunity has yet to present itself. In an unrelated conversation, your mentor tells you about his stressful experience dealing with a deadline that involved 20 colleagues. He outlines the implications and pressure he felt if he didn't deliver on time. By hearing his story and knowing a bit about him, you can thereby *imagine* working in a similar environment. Upon prodding a bit further, you can determine some of the necessary qualities needed to be successful in a similar scenario. Once you understand what it takes to be successful, you can speak on such a topic (to a recruiter or future boss, perhaps) as if you truly *experienced* it. Just by listening, you gain this real-world experience and "hands-off" knowledge. However, when the time comes and you're faced with a similar decision, be strategic in your response. Don't simply replicate the scenario because it's what you've heard. Do what makes sense for you and the position, and applies to your own skill set and personality.

Beyond "collecting" experience vis a vis the stories of others, strategic listening helps others see you as a confidant. While I can't pinpoint when exactly this happens with most of my relationships, my experience tells me that asking poignant questions, being generally enthusiastic, ascribing to a certain level of informality, and exuding humility leads the storyteller to trust me. When you gain someone's trust, you've laid the fundamentals down for a worthwhile and fruitful professional relationship.

LEAVE A FAVORABLE IMPRESSION

Sometimes listening is difficult if the person across from us happens to be insufferable. Perhaps this is your first time meeting him or her and you instantly find them off-putting. We will undoubtedly encounter these people as we progress in our careers. Due to no fault of your own, he or she might simply be contentious, condescending, or arrogant. However, despite how painful the conversation may be, the key is to maintain your composure and continue giving the other person your full attention and time.

Here's a hypothetical scenario to give this idea some context: Imagine you are considering joining a startup but aren't entirely sure the product is going to succeed (although one could argue such uncertainty is felt at every startup). At the same time, you've recently met with someone who is fairly successful in his respective field, and he asks about your career plans. You mention your misgivings about the startup, and he tells you not to join the company because of various reasons: the chance it fails, leaving a secure corporate job, etc. Rather than engage this naysayer and counter his beliefs, it will behoove you to listen anyway, letting him know you will take his opinion into consideration. Even if he eventually sees that you didn't take his advice, you still leave a favorable impression with him. If you instead push back and argue his opinion, the only impression you leave him with is of an argumentative and unappreciative millennial whom he won't likely want to see again or help.

There's no need to be combative when someone provides a differing opinion or disagreeable advice. This is especially true if you request the meeting, as your contact assumes you want their perspective. Regardless of whether you care to see this person again, remember he or she went out of their way to provide you counsel. The least you can do is listen in return. Burning a bridge reaps zero benefit.

While you are never beholden to anybody else's opinion or judgment but your own, you will be judged if you are perceived to be a poor listener. Oddly enough, most people don't remember the specific advice they provide someone, anyway. What they will remember, however, is whether that person was attentive and appreciative of their time.

Continue seeking the advice and counsel of others whenever and wherever you can. And no matter how objectionable, don't contradict someone else's opinion that you invited. Just listen to it. Humility is like the infamous tortoise; it will outlast pride (i.e., the hare) over and over again.

THE BENEFITS OF BEING AN EXCELLENT LISTENER

GAIN FRESH
PERSPECTIVE
•
LEAVES A
FAVORABLE IMPRESSION

MAKE UP FOR
YOUR INEXPERIENCE
•
ADVANCES A
CONVERSATION

DEVELOP YOUR LISTENING ABILITY

Because I love to talk, I constantly work on being silent when someone else is speaking. Some conversations—and people—are easier to listen to than others, but there are a few core actions I take in every conversation. These steps have and continue to help me develop my listening ability:

- **Place my phone out of sight:** If you're expecting an important call or email, and you must have your phone out, set it face down with the ringer on low (and turn your texts on silent). It's too easy to get distracted and glance at our phones when we see or hear various alerts. If a meeting is of particular importance, you may want to leave your phone in the car or put it on "do not disturb" (for iPhones) so no sound emanates from it. If I've left it in the car, I might even mention it to the contact so he or she knows they have my undivided attention.

- **Bring a notepad and pen:** I learned this from my journalist days, and now I never attend a meeting without these two items. I take notes at every sit-down conversation I have for multiple reasons, most of which are obvious. One that might not be is because my contact seems generally more enthusiastic about giving me their time. Sometimes I'll even interject their dialogue with a "Wow, I'm writing that one down!" to emphasize that I'm listening, and that I find the speaker's advice or experience useful. Even if I never look at the notes after that initial meeting, I will remember the general premise of our meeting because I have gone through the act of writing down the highlights.

- **Maintain eye contact:** During your very next conversation with someone, notice how often the person looks directly at you while speaking. Making eye contact is critical to building a relationship. According to a study by communications-analytics company Quantified Communications, adults only make eye contact 30–60 percent of the time, yet 60–70 percent is key to creating a sense of emotional connection.[7] I remember once being at a breakfast with a well-known tennis broadcaster. The conversation was impromptu and informal, as there were a couple of others at the table. But for whatever reason, he would not look anybody in the eye. It was the most bizarre thing! Those at the table simply looked at one another confused, and after a few minutes, we all acted as if he wasn't there so we could continue speaking comfortably. Avoiding someone's eyes can make others feel unappreciated, insignificant, or just generally confused, so always maintain eye contact. While the above study suggests direct contact about 70 percent of the time, I personally shoot for 80–90 percent of the time, as I find the conversation is typically more thought-provoking or I'm generally more engaged.

However, one could argue that locking eyes with someone can seem off-putting, so use your best judgment. To break up the eye contact (and get to that 10 percent), I will reach for a glass of water or adjust my jacket.

- **Ask impromptu questions:** Whether you're interviewing for a position or meeting a new contact, ask at least one impromptu question. Generic questions (e.g., "how did you get into this field" or "what do you like most about your job") are fine to move the conversation along, but an unstructured, spur-of-the-moment question can strengthen your interaction and expand the discussion. As your contact is speaking and something interesting comes to mind, speak up. Some people are afraid of interrupting, but if you interject ever so politely with a related question—or if something is unclear—he or she won't be offended. Perhaps you're stuck on what to ask? That's when your note-taking can help. Have you written anything down from the conversation? If so, bring up a note you jotted down and turn that into a question whenever there is a lull or silence. If you can get into the habit of taking small notes as a conversation unfolds, then following up with impromptu questions will also become second nature.

CHAPTER FIVE

DETERMINE YOUR FATE

*"It is not necessary to accept the choices
handed down to you by life as you know it."*

-Hunter S. Thompson

MANY PEOPLE STRIVE to find the perfect job. Call me cynical, but I don't know if such a thing exists. There are definitely jobs out there that are better than others, and my cynicism doesn't mean we stop trying to find that ideal career, one that combines both our passions and interests. But the likelihood that the perfect career exists *and* that it pays well is, well, very slim.

That said, there is a silver lining: most people hate their jobs. So, if you like your job more than 60 percent of the time, you're probably happier than the majority of the workforce. Why 60 percent? Well if you like your job 50 percent of the time, that means you also dislike it the same amount of time. Still, a bad workday or workweek is inevitable. Perhaps a given assignment isn't challenging, your manager is not treating you well, or you took the blame for a coworker's mistake. We all have those days. Hopefully, those bad days don't occur as much or more than the good ones. If you're finding that they're becoming a regularity—as in you like your job 40 percent of the time or less—then you may need to rethink your current position or career path.

So, if you dislike your job more often than you enjoy it, there are three general career directions you can take.

1. You can quit your current job,

2. You can get a new job, or

3. You can change careers.

Please note: each option follows many of the same initial steps and exploratory phases. Feel free to skip to the section that best relates to your desired path.

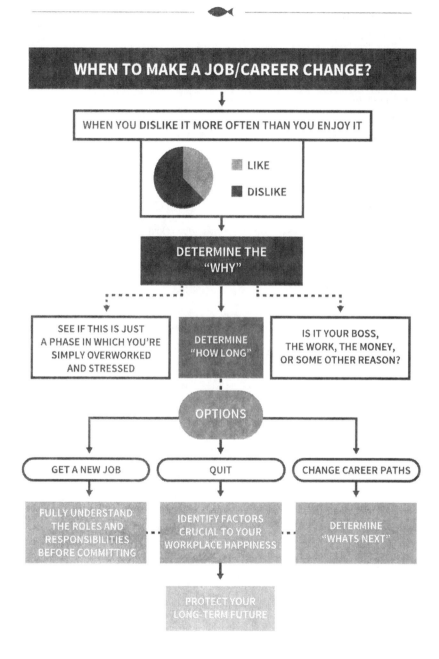

1. YOU QUIT YOUR CURRENT JOB

If your salaried job becomes so unbearable that you would rather take an hourly wage at a yoga studio or coffee shop, then sometimes there is no better option than to quit.

I've always been told never to quit a job until I have a backup job, or some other source of income, lined up. This is a "should" I strongly oppose. You can quit a job whenever you feel compelled; but if you do quit, protect your long-term future by exiting your current workplace the *right way*. You can still leave on your own terms, but you must:

- Do "right" by everybody you've encountered, especially your managers so you never "burn a bridge."

- Be visibly appreciative of everyone your last few days, even if you barely interacted with him or her while you worked there.

- Be remembered for exerting as great, if not greater, an effort in your last days than when you first came aboard.

- Be as genuine and sincere as humanly possible, even as you take your final exit through those office doors.

I know that following these steps is the best way to quit a job because I've done so—three times. All exits were not perfect, but the second was better than the first, and the third was better than the second. Beyond simply growing up, each departure improved, since I did not want any one thing I did or said to overshadow my work product.

Before I delve further into my exit strategy, I suggest you first figure out exactly *why* you want to quit. While the reason(s) may not always be straightforward, it's critical that you analyze the why rather than rush into a decision. Also, when you *do* quit, everyone will ask you why, including your future employer. And if you don't speak assuredly about your reason(s), you give others a reason to doubt you.

So, why do you want to quit? Give this some real, considerable thought. Here are a few exploratory questions: Which aspects of your current job do you dislike? On that same note, what do you find absolutely intolerable? Could it be your boss? The actual work? If it's the work, what don't you like? Is there any enjoyment you derive from the work? If so, can you see yourself doing that small activity throughout your *entire* workday? If the answer to that last question is a yes, or at least a maybe, then perhaps you just need to have a conversation with your manager about how you can work on more of what you enjoy and less on what you don't.

Still, even after shifting your role or responsibilities, most (if not all) jobs come with unpleasant tasks. And while you need to like your job at least 60 percent of the time no matter what you're working on, sometimes the work is menial simply because you are in a lower-level position. If you are in an entry or mid-level position and dislike the work you're doing, do the job duties of your boss, or your boss' boss, seem appealing? Do their jobs excite you even a little, beyond the shiny title and pay raise? Could you see yourself in a similar role some day? If you answered yes to any of those questions, you might just be a bit burned out on your current work. Burnout is common your first couple of years in a job, especially if you're young in your career, working long hours, and doing the same activities in which you started. So, if your boss allows you to take on more projects that you find enjoyable, then ride it out. Eventually, after "putting in your time," you'll be that much closer to where your boss is today.

However, sometimes the amount of time you "put in" is irrelevant, and a company only hires externally for certain level positions. Also, the appropriate amount of "time" in a given job is relative these days. While the general rule of thumb is at least one year, everyone has their own reason for leaving, or story to tell. In today's workforce, professional happiness is more important than job security. Some companies certainly appreciate and reward loyalty, signified by years of continued service, but remember it's *your time* being spent, and only you can best determine the quality of that time.

To explain further, if you strive to make an immediate impact at a new job, you don't need to have worked for a company for three years before you are considered a valuable asset. The following guidelines are probably not revolutionary, but it's the sum of all the below tactics that help someone speed up their learning curve and quickly become a highly-regarded employee:

- **Work long hours.** Don't subscribe to the 9–5. You don't have to be the first one in the office (unless you're a morning person), but strive to be the last one to leave. Beyond being recognized as a hard worker, working long hours quickly allows you to become immersed in the ins and outs of the organization. Also, the more you work, the greater your bandwidth, so you can take on additional projects and gain exposure to more people.

- **Take on more than your core responsibilities.** By volunteering for projects outside of your day-to-day role, you not only gain exposure to new colleagues but you also experience other business units within your company, enhancing your overall work experience. Moreover, by taking on alternative work, you thereby develop new skills, which can be worthwhile adds to your résumé.

- **Meet with and talk to as many people as possible.** Whether you begin a small conversation with someone in the company kitchen, in the elevator on the way into work, or at a company outing, always express interest in other people and their stories. Building internal relationships will quickly allow you to feel more invested in the company. Also, getting immediately acquainted with your colleagues helps you build staying power. If you know more people, it appears as if you've been employed longer—when you can bridge conversations and make introductions yourself. To that end, I learn about my colleagues by asking different questions, such as, "How long have you been at the company?" or "What are your job duties?" If they aren't responsive or friendly, I won't further pry. However, people generally enjoy talking about themselves and don't usually seem bothered if I try to get to know them. Note: if you work for a startup or smaller company — as is the exception to many of this book's suggestions — this tip might not be entirely relevant, as you're already working with the majority of your coworkers on a weekly basis. This tactic becomes more challenging when working for a larger organization with hundreds of employees.

Let's go back to the "why"—or your reason(s) for wanting to quit. Perhaps you want to leave because of your boss. He or she isn't interested in your personal development, doesn't have your best interests in mind, is inappropriate or condescending, or isn't helping you learn or grow. If any of these possibilities ring true, can you get another boss? A great friend and mentor once gave me the following piece of advice: If your boss stinks, well that stinks; but if your boss' boss also stinks, then you *need* to look elsewhere for a job because neither of your supervisors is going to be concerned about your well-being or advancement. Over 75 percent of millennials wish their managers were more supportive, like a coach, according to the mentorship app Betterup.[8] Managers take things out on their direct reports all the time. You've seen the movies or heard the horror stories. Maybe your manager has low self-esteem, is jealous, or feels threatened by you in some capacity? Who knows why he or she acts the way they do—the reason is not your concern. Instead, look out for yourself and attempt to change your bad luck by getting a new boss.

Or maybe it's not the boss that's bringing you down but the work environment. No matter where you work or in what industry, getting along with coworkers is crucial to enjoying your work, especially when collaborating on projects or assignments. According to Forbes, a company's culture is seen as one of the top factors contributing to workplace happiness; sometimes even more than one's salary.[9] Do you not like or get along with your coworkers? Or is the culture just a bit off, one in which you don't think you can thrive? To that end, I ask, "Could it be *you*?" If you aren't sure of the answer to any of these questions, test out different approaches in the office and see whether anything resonates better with your colleagues. We typically spend all day with our coworkers, and while it's important to always act appropriately and politely (or HR will come calling), we don't always want to be "on." Sometimes we just want to be ourselves. Typically, the smaller a company, the more informal/ casual the culture, where everyone is friends and gets together outside of work. Those environments are fun and productive for some companies. But if your company is a bit larger and more formal, making friends with your colleagues might not be possible. Determine how important a company's culture is to you, especially as you apply to your next job.

Sometimes, the reason you're dissatisfied at work is all about the Benjamins. Maybe your salary remains unchanged, despite the life responsibilities you've accrued over the years (marriage, mortgage, etc). Maybe you've been at the company for a few years and your boss committed to giving you a specific increase in your compensation, or a title promotion, but nothing has come. If you've tried to talk to your boss about it and see no progress made, I'm afraid you were granted invisible promises. I've been there. During negotiations with a prior employer, my then-boss committed to a title and salary promotion after a six-month review. After seven months, I recalled the arrangement, only to find out the company had a policy against promoting its employees within one year of service. While that instance wasn't what led me to quit, it caused me to distrust my boss going forward and be aware of future false promises.

If a promotion wasn't promised, you may have to stomach a smaller salary now in the hopes of a more lucrative future. If you feel as though you are being severely underpaid, have a conversation with your supervisor or Human Resources so you can better understand what steps you need to take to get to that next level of compensation. Be sure to exhaust your resources and ask all the necessary questions before you give up hope of receiving additional monies.

If none of the above are reasons why you want to quit, and you're relying more on feeling than rationale, perhaps you could speak to a career counselor or therapist to gain more insight. I did, and I found it extremely helpful. Talking to an objective source—not a parent, friend, or mentor—provides a unique perspective on your situation, including any harsh realities you may not be admitting or are avoiding. Maybe you're actually making the job out to be worse than it is!

After all, your job is still a "job." It's not supposed to be full of rainbows and daily happy hours. Good jobs will challenge you, force you to learn and grow, and help you better understand what you enjoy doing (or not doing). Regardless of your reason for disliking your job, you are still learning about yourself, which helps you develop into a more mature person (and professional).

"Good jobs will challenge you, force you to learn and grow, and help you better understand what you enjoy doing (or not doing)."

That said, if you've taken all the necessary steps to understand exactly why you don't like your job, including exhausting all your resources, then you should feel *good* about quitting—because whatever is to come will undoubtedly be greater than what you are leaving behind.

2. YOU GET A NEW JOB

If you took option 1 (and quit), hopefully you reach option 2 (and get a new job) quickly afterward, as I hear unemployment checks aren't that lucrative. Better yet, maybe you'll take this option directly and transition into a new job from your previous one. For whatever reason (identified using the rationale discussed in option 1 as a guide), you've decided to leave your current workplace. You may not quit outright, but you are no longer happy and are certain you want to work for a different company. While the perfect work situation or job may not exist, let's make sure the next place you work is at least more enjoyable than your last. To accomplish this, identify the factors crucial to your professional enjoyment *now*, and carry these priorities with you to your next job. In other words, what are the positives, or "pros," of your current job? Is it the flexible hours? The casual environment? Write down the top two or three qualities (if you're lucky to have that many, maybe your situation isn't that bad after all) that enhance your job, and remember them as you interview elsewhere. *And don't bend on these qualities—prioritize them.* If a potential employer doesn't have the factors you know contribute to your happiness, keep looking until you find them, in addition to hopefully a few other positives, somewhere else.

Sometimes, though, there aren't enough work perks in the world to make up for the actual work you'll be doing. I've talked to several people who get hired for a job with roles and responsibilities explicitly outlined, but, once they start, they end up doing completely different work. I've been there, too. Working on assignments in a role for which you didn't initially sign up may not be ideal, as you're probably operating out of your comfort zone. Still, it could prove valuable if you're open-minded. Some might see this new role as an opportunity to become more well-rounded and knowledgeable—and potentially more desirable in the marketplace, as you're expanding your skill set and gaining additional tools. But to those of you who just want to do what you expected and what you know you enjoy, you may hate your new job more than your last. So, before you accept their offer, get a crystal clear picture of what your day-to-day will look like.

The formal job description might be a good starting point in determining your expected responsibilities. If you are able to obtain this (common for jobs posted online and less so for word-of-mouth positions), discount the positives by a quarter. It's likely a job will never be as great as it reads. If the job seems really great, it's probably still pretty good, but not nearly as good as the description. Some job descriptions are incredibly vague and don't really explain what you would be doing. That doesn't mean you wouldn't like the job per se, but rather the job description is repurposed for several similar positions. Regardless, most people will oversell a position. Remember we're talking about a job here, not an all-expenses paid trip to Paris! Try to be discerning when interviewing or examining a job description, identifying any responsibilities you might find unpleasant. If you were to accept the job, would you be comfortable performing those "unpleasant" tasks? Imagine if you were only tasked with the responsibilities you perceived to be negatives. Just for a minute, picture yourself doing those tasks on a day-to-day basis. Do you think you could still find enjoyment in the job, if those disagreeable tasks became the bulk of your workload?

It's important to put yourself in all sorts of shoes when you are about to accept a new job, and to think about whether you could be happy there. Because you aren't just putting on a new pair of shoes; you will own those shoes for the foreseeable future. Ultimately, a job description is useful at a high level. However, if you're close to taking a position, current employees of the company or the hiring manager are your best references to clear up any ambiguity. Most jobs are filled after several rounds of interviews. Ask different questions of each employee to get a better sense of the work they do, if they enjoy it, and whether their roles are strictly or loosely defined.

Once you've been hired somewhere, you then have to go through the awkwardness of leaving your *current* job. This is a weird event for which you cannot prepare. You'll rarely speak to the people you bumped into every day; what has become a familiar scene will soon be a distant memory. You may have some doubts when you leave, especially as you say your goodbyes, because there's uncertainty ahead. But it's also an incredibly exciting time. Focus on why you're leaving and *what* you're venturing into, and any momentary sadness will eventually subside. As long as you leave in a manner as polite and respectful as the day you came in, nobody can blame you for wanting to better your situation. If you do right by your colleagues until the very last minute of your tenure, then they can only speak highly of you.

3. YOU CHANGE CAREERS

Maybe you don't simply want to quit your job or leave your current employer; you want to make a more drastic change and venture into a new career field. If this an idea you've contemplated, do you know what path you next want to take? Also, are you certain that the field in which you currently work is not the field you want to be in going forward?

Ultimately, it's a tricky question: *How do we know what we want to do for the rest of our lives?*

For some people, the answer is straightforward. Those who went to medical or law school, for instance, have focused career paths. The rest of us, who majored in disciplines like business or liberal arts, have career paths that are seemingly less certain. But there are advantages to both kinds of paths. The sociology major isn't worse off than the engineer; one path might just take a little longer to reach his or her ideal career. On the other hand, sometimes the person that spent all that time and money in school, on one linear path, decides he or she wants a different career after all.

Regardless of where you are in your career and your life, fortunately you never have to stay there. Many people are afraid they'll take a step backward if they change careers. Ironically, what these people fail to realize is that making a change is actually a step forward, toward a happier, more rewarding place. They're scared to lose the incremental salary and/or benefits that come with putting in their time somewhere. But if somebody isn't feeling fulfilled in his or her career, no amount of bonuses or promotions can fake one's professional happiness.

THE "WHY" AND "HOW LONG"

If you are one of those people who has question a career change but has yet to take action, ask yourself some of the same exploratory questions posited in option 1 (You Quit):

- Examine the "why," to truly understand the reason you want to change careers. Answering this can help you mitigate your risk in the chance that your discontent is only temporary. Sometimes we mistake a particular aspect of the job or company (e.g., boss, work culture, organizational structure, etc.) as a reason we no longer enjoy that career path.

- Examine "how long," to better understand the duration of your unhappiness. As previously mentioned, you could simply be overworked and overwhelmed. Take up other interests outside of work, such as a new project or online class. Or take a mini-vacation (even if that means you don't leave your bed; at least you're not at work). Sometimes a personal reset allows you to reprioritize. Determine if either tactic rejuvenates you at all

  Before I transitioned from a career in consulting to business development, I dedicated 30 minutes to writing every night after work. It was a passion project of mine, and something stable I had to look forward to, even if my day-to-day work wasn't enjoyable. Eventually, the sum of my writings became the first draft of this book!

If you can both identify the reason you're making this career change and feel convinced about the decision for some length of time, then you're probably doing the right thing. "Some length of time" is subjective and probably more of a gut-check than any formal timeline. Regardless, deliberating on such a major decision will allow you to move forward with confidence rather than had you done so on a whim.

At one point in my career, I didn't heed the above advice. I got caught up, and failed to examine the "why" or the "how long." As mentioned earlier, I used to be a sports reporter. Because it was my first job— what I thought was a dream job—it absorbed my life. I worked seven days a week for at least 10 hours a day. Eighteen months later, I started disliking the job. A writer by trade, the on-camera assignments slowly became the bulk of my work; and I didn't want to be thought of as just another "pretty face." Once these feelings crept in, I soon questioned the entire field: Did people actually read anymore? Did it even matter what I said, as people only seemed to comment on my appearance? I concluded that my role was too insignificant in the grander scheme of the sports industry. Eventually, the doubts hit a breaking point. I talked myself out of the thing I loved most in the world (writing about sports), because it had become the ONLY thing I had in the world. I assumed I was no longer meant to be a journalist and, thus, should permanently leave the field. After a few months of feeling fatigued from my "one love," I quit.

Something I realized only *after* leaving this field was that my core job responsibilities evolved (from writing to on-camera work), and I didn't like the new role as much. I didn't examine the "why" or "how long"—in that I wanted to take on more writing assignments and desperately needed a vacation—*before* I changed careers.

While I successfully transitioned into a different career after journalism, would I have made the same decision back then if I truly understood the root of my frustrations? I don't know that answer now, but it's certainly something I could have more fully explored at the time.

And that's the trouble with making a change: You have to stomach the decision you made, as there's no reversing it. So, make your decisions whole-heartedly, look back sparingly, and welcome the unknown. You are guiding yourself toward a better place, even if you don't know what that world looks like yet.

LinkedIn co-founder Reid Hoffman changed jobs and industries multiple times before creating one of the world's biggest social networks. In his book *The Start-Up of You*, Hoffman explains that there's hardly ever a "right" time to make such a change:

> When is it time to change divisions, change jobs, or even change
> the industry you work in? You'll rarely know for sure when to pivot
> or when to persist in what you're doing. In general, a lesson from
> the technology industry is that it's better to be in front of a big
> change than to be behind it....what you're doing now doesn't have
> to be failing for it to make sense to shift.[10]

Some of you won't feel doubt. Sometimes you are so certain of your next path that you don't need to deliberate any longer. Your gut simply knows. In those rare cases, your excitement for the future and confidence in your upcoming success propels you to take a leap of faith. Still, it doesn't hurt to talk through your rationale with friends and family. Even if you don't heed their advice, it can be worthwhile to hear what those closest to you—those who have your best-interests in mind—think.

[10] www.amazon.com/The-Start-up-You-Yourself-Transform-ebook/dp/B0050DIWHU

Ultimately, if you make too drastic of a change, you might later end up doubting or even regretting your decision. Just ask any entrepreneur. The most successful business owners are those who balance the proper amount of risk with an equivalent measure of caution. They manage their expectations against their desires. If the change you're considering could be too risky, it probably is. Keep your inner circle close at every step as you navigate your own path to happiness, and check in with them when you need a sounding board or second opinion.

THE "WHAT NEXT"

Let's say a career change is imminent for you. You've examined the *why* and *how long* for some time. But what about the "what next," which encompasses two essential questions: "Where are you headed next?" and "Why that particular career field?"

WHERE ARE YOU HEADED NEXT?

Tackling this question isn't as overwhelming as it seems. Rather than get caught up in your career trajectory over the next 10 or 15 years, try thinking in smaller steps. Once you plan your very next step, then decide the very next step after that one. It's never a bad idea to have a larger goal in mind, where you can actually visualize your answer to the almighty "where do you see yourself in XX number of years" question. But some people just don't plan that far ahead, or their dream has evolved, and their once-clear image of the future has now become cloudy. Wherever you fall in that spectrum is up to you; remember, it's *your* future to own. Nobody will hold you responsible for accomplishing your goals but you (and maybe an overzealous parent).

To illustrate, whenever someone asked my 17-year-old self where I would be in 10 or 15 years, I often responded, "Accepting an Oscar for Best Actress." Fast forward nearly 10 years and that idea now sounds ridiculous! While I'm impressed (and simultaneously embarrassed) at my young confidence, I've considered a handful of other careers since that time. My "ideal career" has deviated so much from its original plan that I no longer have one almighty plan. However, as long as I always have an immediate goal in mind, I'm convinced that I'm continuing along an upward trajectory.

Whether your career journey is mapped out or it isn't, hopefully the change you're about to make at least generally aligns to your professional goals. Otherwise you're impulsively making a change, weighing immediate unhappiness more heavily than long-term satisfaction. One factor to consider is that your new career—while it may still help you get to where you want to ultimately go—could delay your long-range goals by a few years. It doesn't always have to, but cracking into a new industry may require you to take a couple steps backward. Who knows — you might change careers yet again, as you continue exploring what you *don't* want to do. While these learnings may initially take some time, you are, at the same time, setting yourself up for the long run. I've spoken to dozens of established professionals who confided that they wished they had the foresight or chutzpah to alter their career paths earlier in life.

WHY THAT PARTICULAR CAREER FIELD?

If you can't pinpoint what field to next venture into but you are certain the previous one wasn't the right fit, here are a few methods to aid you in your exploration:

- What are some of your favorite brands or companies? Is there a website you visit every day? If so, go to that company's job board and check out the listed positions. See if anything posted sounds interesting and/or feels like a good match with your skill set.

- Find out how others figured it out. Get outside and talk to friends, family, colleagues, or anyone you come across and find out how they chose their given field. Listen to their stories. Most people will likely tell you that they didn't know they would end up where they are today. Maybe hearing such responses will validate your indecision, allowing you to be more open-minded when applying to a new job.

- Attend any kind of event you can. Go to conferences, panel discussions, or tradeshows. A couple helpful websites are www.10times.com or www.meetup.com. Both sites allow you to sort events by industry and location. While these events could be great networking opportunities, don't feel obligated to talk to others if you're still figuring out your next field. Your intention is to learn. If you do engage others, keep your objective in mind. Ask your new contact what their day-to-day entails, or how they like working in that industry.

- Meet with a recruiter or career consultant. A career coach can help match your skills/interests to certain industries.

Online career assessments are, as previously mentioned, also available, although they don't often provide personalized insight. A good recruiter or career consultant keeps a pulse on what is currently in-demand in the market. They might even suggest niche industries and/or positions that you've never heard about, or are too specific to be mentioned in an online assessment.

When I decided to end my journalism career, I abruptly encountered my *what next:* I had neither a job nor any real sense of what I wanted to do. As I mentioned in Chapter 2, I took a little bit of "me time" to solidfy my core skills and strengths and explore alternative occupations. Before this introspection, I only felt one certainty: I wanted to continue working in the sports industry. While that belief was somewhat helpful, it didn't really root me in any one career path. Once I defined my skill set, I tried to identify alternative careers within sports that utilized many of my strengths. After conversing with others, attending random networking events, and researching various jobs online, there were a handful of roles I thought I could do well. The trouble was that only one of those career paths sounded appealing at the time, and I didn't have any sort of background in it.

Perhaps you find yourself in a similar predicament, where you are inexperienced or unknowledgeable about an industry, yet are inclined to work in the field. If so, it's important to identify why this new field seems any better than your current industry. What are you expecting to like about it? Do you know anybody working in this industry that can provide you with some insight?

In my case, I expected sports marketing to continue utilizing my communication and analytical skills, but in a less intense manner than being on-camera or in the media. Before I made the leap, I spent ample time talking to various people who worked in marketing, including marketers who worked in different industries. From those conversations, I reasoned that the biggest difference between the fields of journalism and marketing was more conceptual than tactical; I would be communicating on behalf of some*thing* or some*one*, instead of myself.

Just as you identified the duration of your unhappiness in your last job, identify the length of time you've considered this new career path. If only for a short time, that's perfectly normal. Hopefully, however, when you did stumble upon it, it hit you like a ton of bricks. Excuse the "should" I'm about to drop, but this is significant: you should never jump careers if the one you desire doesn't appear to be more worthwhile than your current field. What I mean by "worthwhile" is a career that will draw upon both your passions and strengths, excites you, and seems rewarding or significant in some way. Rarely are you going to feel all of those things every single day at a job, but that's the goal, anyway. So strive for a job that appears to be worthwhile. Because if you jump for jump's sake, you'll likely end up as unsettled and unhappy as you were before you left.

TRANSFERABLE SKILLS

Now you've understood, or are closer to understanding, the *why*, *how long*, and *what next*. That's a great start. But you're not done yet. You can't just change careers because you've figured out why you want to leave, how long it took you to determine, and where you want to go next. In order to successfully change careers—that is, to convince others that you will excel in your prospective field—

you'll need to demonstrate **transferable skills**. In other words, what skills do you currently possess that enable your success elsewhere? Do any of your skills or interests align to a potential job that you've come across? How can you prove to a possible employer that your past *helped* you get to this point, rather than hindered you?

"Skills are much more powerful than experience because skills are versatile; job experience tends to be limited by the position, field, or situation."

It's important to identify your transferable skills because the specific job functions and tasks you handled at your last post will likely be very different from those of your desired career. People often mistake prior experience for skills learned, but the two are not at all the same. Skills are much more powerful than experience because skills are versatile; job experience tends to be limited by the position, field, or situation. Most importantly, you are the owner of your skills, while a title is a few words someone arbitrarily ascribed to you. You can always teach yourself new skills, separate from whatever skills you develop within a given role.

By re-framing your job materials (résumé, cover letter, portfolio, etc.) to reflect your transferable skills, a career change doesn't seem as far-fetched as it otherwise could. If, on the other hand, you merely list prior job titles and don't allude to your transferable skills, you may appear unqualified. Most people won't spend time dissecting your résumé wondering whether you'll be able to succeed in a different role. You have to make the connection for them; consider it part of your presentation to a potential employer. Illustrate your capabilities both in person and on paper.

So, take out that résumé and examine it. By each job title you've held, jot down any skills you've developed. For example, were you an assistant at a movie studio? Great. Then you don't just have "assistant experience," but you could also be organized, detail-oriented, and intimately knowledgeable about the entertainment industry. If you were an engineer but are looking to become an investment banker, maybe you could discuss how you volunteered to manage the P & L reports on a project, thereby possessing budget management skills.

If you get the chance to explain your situation in-person, your ultimate litmus test will be how much confidence you display. If you believe that your skills are valuable and transferrable, then you don't "lack experience," but instead have atypical experience. If you are equipped with the same ability to perform in this field as a current employee of the company, but happened to develop those skills elsewhere — state as much. Exuding self-confidence will be your key to a seamless career transition. Most people understand leaving a career that doesn't ladder up to your passions. But nobody will believe you can be a rockstar and perform at a high level if *you* don't.

During her commencement speech at Harvard, actress Natalie Portman echoed a similar sentiment, confessing that her first opportunity to direct a film arose only because people thought she could:

My complete ignorance as to my own limitations looked like
confidence, and got me into the director's chair. Once there, I had
to figure it all out. And my belief that I could handle these things,
contrary to all evidence of my ability to do so, was half the battle.
The other half was very hard work. [11]

Portman's clout arguably worked in her favor, but you, too, can open
doors for yourself by conveying similar confidence. It worked for me,
and nobody will likely ask me to speak at Harvard. When I left the field
of journalism to pursue a career in marketing, I imagined getting a job
would be nearly impossible. And if not impossible, certainly getting
the job would take some time. But, in the vein of taking risks, I took
another and moved to New York to expand my search. There were
many more opportunities in New York than Los Angeles at the time.
In early October, I bought a round-trip ticket from Los Angeles to New
York, with plans to come back to LA for Thanksgiving. I gave myself
six weeks to get hired; in case I came up empty-handed, I would move
back home. Truthfully, I only had enough money to last me six weeks.
Fortunately, I only had to wait four. By early November, I was offered an
entry-level marketing role at a major sports television network. Before
I received the offer, I underwent several rounds of interviews. Over a
three-week period, I met with a total of eight people at the company.
That's not a typo. And nearly every interviewer asked about my lack
of marketing experience. I presumed I'd be asked the question, so I
prepared in two ways:

- First, I did my best to authentically "talk the talk." Every industry
  uses its own acronyms and verbiage. So, a few days prior to each
  interview, I researched and memorized marketing jargon. I then

embedded a few of the words I'd picked up into my conversations. My objective in including these buzz words was two-fold:
I wanted to a) demonstrate that I was a quick study. Thus, whatever I didn't know then I would soon learn; and, b) stress that,
while inexperienced in the technical sense, I understood the field
adequately enough to perform well in the role (when in reality,
I had no clue what I was doing!).

- Second, rather than focus on why I wasn't qualified, I instead
highlighted my transferrable skills. I proudly discussed the skills
I'd learned and developed as a journalist and how they would
shape me into a great marketer. I never mentioned not having
enough experience, changing career fields, being green to
marketing, etc. If any of those details came up, I addressed them
casually and quickly. I hoped that my entire presentation and
preparation would be remembered more than those details—
which, fortunately, did not turn out to be *deal breakers*.

By strategically leveraging (a buzzword in marketing) industry jargon
and highlighting my applicable skills, the "buts" became an after-
thought and the concerns eventually dissipated. The only remaining
question was, "when can you start?" My then-boss was admittedly
picky, and she spent more than six months interviewing candidates.
I half-jokingly say the team was too exhausted to interview anyone
else. While the opportunity certainly came at the "right time and right
place," I still seized it by expressing confidence in my capabilities.
Once I received the offer and learned about their painstaking interview
process, I made it my mission to prove that I was the best possible hire
they could have found.

Realistically, changing careers isn't as difficult if you're applying to entry or junior-level positions. Typically, if a job requires three or less years of experience, you can "fake it until you make it." "Faking it" in this context means researching the field and doing your homework to make up for your inexperience, while also selling your transferable skills. Once you get hired, you've successfully "faked it." After that point, strive to "make it." Take whatever necessary steps you may need (webinars, courses, tutorials, books, etc.) to prove to your new employer that they made the right call by taking a chance on you.

CHAPTER SIX

BE A GREAT COLLEAGUE

"Motivation comes from working on things we care about. It also comes from working with people we care about."

— Sheryl Sandberg

MAINTAIN A POSITIVE ENERGY

Have you ever had a coworker who seemed to make your job more enjoyable? Separate from an office romance or working with a best friend, there are certain people who generally improve an office environment. Maybe you can't necessarily pinpoint why this person makes work more pleasant, but he or she brings a positive energy that is welcomed amidst the stuffiness of Corporate America. This kind of positively energetic person is a valuable commodity at work. Strive to be this person for your colleagues and maintain a positive energy.

"Energy" here is not referred to in an ethereal or holistic sense. Rather, a positively energetic person in this context emanates "energy," literally. At the same time, I preface energy with the adjective "positive," because some high-motored people can rub others the wrong way. You want to find a balance between being energetic enough that you incite action, conversation, and collaboration among your colleagues, while also controlling your energy so it doesn't distract others. If you can become a positively energetic person at work, and maintain that attitude on a day-to-day basis, it will benefit you wherever you work. Here are a few reasons why:

- When brainstorming with a smaller team, people will feed off your energy, enabling new ideas to more easily come to mind. Sometimes, everyone has a "case of the Mondays" and is too tired to think outside the box. Your positive energy can help wake everyone up and increase the collective's productivity.

- If you consistently maintain a positive energy, others will find and give you work. Often times, when employees are bogged down with work, they resort to being short with colleagues. By working efficiently while always finding time to be nice to others, people will notice the clip and fervency at which you work, which can open the door to new responsibilities or assignments.

- A positive energy is palpable. Typically, a smile evokes another person's smile, or a compliment encourages brief conversation. If you greet your floor with a "good morning," for instance, your colleagues are forced to look up from their screens and recognize the people around them, hopefully acknowledging you and others with a "good morning" in return. If you can put people in a better mood, most people will want to be around you or will be eager to help you when in need.

- I enjoy my job more. When I invest time to learn about the people around me, I learn more about the company in the process. I'm thereby increasing my own satisfaction at work since I don't feel like just another employee, monotonously clocking in and out. This point is directed at those who tend to complain about a company's poor work culture—if you haven't first tried to change the culture *yourself*, then stop whining!

Maintaining a positive outlook is not always feasible. We're human, after all. Life events happen that don't always make us want to smile. Nonetheless, exhibiting consistent positivity day in and day out will rub off on your coworkers, whether they're conscious of it or not. And that energy has the power to inject a happier disposition across the entire floor, or company if we work at it enough. Here's a few ways I practice maintaining a positive energy at work:

- Rain or shine, I always greet whomever I pass on my way to my desk. It's usually "good morning" or "hello." I'll do the same whenever a coworker or I leave for the day.

- If I'm in the kitchen or elevator, I always strike up a conversation with a colleague. Usually, I ask about his or her weekend, or how work has been going. Call it small talk, but my coworker is usually responsive when I reach out first.

- I ask questions about other people's work. A lot. Even if their work is unrelated to mine. People are usually flattered if you're inquiring about their work, as others tend to be too busy to notice. Sometimes they wonder why you care, but if you ask the question with a compliment, this might yield better results. For instance, I might ask someone whether he or she has any time to walk me through their most recent project, as I've heard a lot of people say it was impressive. Or if a colleague is generally known to produce good work, I'll let him or her know that others think highly of them. If you're humble and complimentary, it's hard for a coworker to tell you "no"—especially when they see you every day.

- I try to inject some humor or a piece of news into a silent room. You've probably been in a situation where you're sitting directly across from a coworker and neither of you say a word all day! Not only is that uncomfortable for you both, but that's not an environment that contributes to professional happiness, collaboration, or positivity. Fill that silence every so often to liven up an ordinarily dispirited day.

HOW TO BE A GREAT COLLEAGUE

BE REFERABLE   •   MAINTAIN A POSITIVE ENERGY

EXUDE SILENT CONFIDENCE   •   ASK SMART QUESTIONS

KEEP YOUR PRIVATE LIFE PRIVATE

BECOME A PRIVATE PERSON

Every company comes with a different kind of culture. I've worked at four companies (and interned at several others) and no culture has been exactly alike. At two of those companies, the culture was incredibly friendly, and I often spent time with colleagues outside of work.

But I've also worked at a company that fell on the opposite side of the work-culture spectrum, where colleagues simply responded, "good" if someone asked, "How was your weekend?"

Before I started working at an incredibly friendly and collaborative startup, I would have suggested to you to head toward the private end of that work-culture spectrum. While it might be fruitful to be a private person no matter where you work, it's worth noting that not all companies are cutthroat or isolating. Still, here are a few reasons why it's generally a good thing to keep your private life private:

- People are competitive. If you supply a coworker with *too* much information about you – such as getting drunk on a weeknight, or lying about calling in sick – they can use what you say against you. While that type of environment or person would have to be extremely cruel/damaging, why even delve into that kind of information at work? If you're out at a work event maybe you can showcase more of your personality and interests, but when you're in the office, keep the conversations professional and appropriate.

- Keeping a clean social media presence is essential to maintaining not only the respect of your colleagues, but also of your professionalism. If you post on social platforms unfettered, you can't control how your message is perceived. People can thus make all sorts of assumptions and judgments about you. Wouldn't you rather be the bearer of your own identity and let someone learn about you – through you? If you're too embarrassed to share a photo that has the potential to be viewed by your boss someday, you probably shouldn't post it on social media.

- When your dating life is an open forum, your openness becomes problematic if you ever become romantically involved with a coworker. Prior to my seriously dating a colleague, I common joked about the struggles of being single. Once our relationship got serious, the single jokes stopped. But my coworkers, thinking I was still single, continued to ask questions. I was forced to lie to keep our relationship secret, and I then had to remember my lies. For someone who takes prides in my integrity, it was an uncomfortable time. Ultimately I would caution against ever dating a colleague, but I'm here to provide career advice, not dating advice. The good news is that if you're already a private person at work, you won't need to make up any stories about your dating life, or backtrack on any things you've said. People will know you don't discuss those topics, anyway.

- When you know too much about somebody, you might un- or subconsciously leak it to another. You may have benevolent intentions while passing along information about one of your colleagues to another colleague. Whether valid or not, that dialogue can be perceived as gossip. The last thing you want to be known for at work is a gossip. Every company has one or more employees that share too much. Don't fall into their trap of sharing back an equal amount. You want to be remembered by others for your work product, work ethic, or positive demeanor – not that you were the one that found out Stacy was getting fired.

You might think maintaining a positive energy at work contradicts being a private person, but it actually doesn't; you can be both. The thing to be cautious of is how much you indulge or offer up, whether that information is communicated online or in-person. Also, when you ask questions or engage with others, keep the focus on work, or the topics light and positive.

EARN THE RESPECT OF OTHERS

Over time, I've found that gaining others' respect in the workplace is best achieved two ways: by asking smart questions and exuding silent confidence:

1. **Asking smart questions** is a skill I've fine-tuned over time; frankly, I'm still developing it. While I've always been an incredibly curious person (my parents' grey hairs are testament), there are times when asking a question *just because* I'm curious isn't appropriate. Let your intuition guide the situation. Understand when a question might be well-received and when it's best to either look it up yourself or ask it at a later time. Sometimes, asking questions (that we *think* are smart) gives the impression as if we're trying to prove something.
Depending on the objective, maybe you are intentionally trying to prove yourself. But there are circumstances when intentionally asking a question can do more harm than good.

   – For example, say you end up in a meeting with one or more of your company's executives. If you don't get exposure to people at this level often, asking a question might help you get noticed. And if your question is thoughtful, relevant, furthers the discussion, and/or helps identify another gap that needs to be addressed, you're demonstrating your value to the company (as well as your courage).

> Say, on the other hand, you are in a meeting with your smaller internal team. But your CEO also happens to attend the meeting that day. Asking a question that you either already know the answer to or isn't entirely relevant to the discussion will reap little benefit. Your team might assume you are trying to get face time with the boss, rather than helping support the larger goal. Even if that's not the assumption, a tangential question could irritate others because you're zapping precious time away from the meeting. If you do really solid work, the bosses will find out you exist. You don't need to hold up a sign that screams "Notice Me" just because you don't often get those face-to-face opportunities.

2. **Exuding silent confidence** also helps you earn other peoples' respect. But instead of earning it in a short amount of time by asking smart questions, silent confidence gets noticed gradually. I preface "confidence" with the word "silent" because, in order to earn the respect of others, your work and actions must do all the talking. A silently confident person completes their work with little to no complaint, and offers to help others with their work—without informing anybody that they took such initiative. Also, this person continues to work until the work is complete, striving to exceed the expectations of the recipient

or requestor, even if that means staying late or working on the weekends. At the core of the silently confident person is their work ethic. They work without expectation of praise or recognition. They do it foremost for themselves and because their name is on the work, and only hope it meets the approval of others thereafter.

- However, sometimes you may never earn a colleague's respect, particularly when a company's culture favors politics over hard work. While this is not as common as it probably once was (i.e., when CEOs resigned and gave an undeserving son the reigns), being validated is critical to most people's professional worth. If you are never recognized for your painstaking efforts, perhaps you shop around to a company that will applaud your hard work.

BE WORTHY OF A RECOMMENDATION

When you're a great colleague, you'll always have great references. Before you can get a coworker to write you a letter of recommendation, though, you'll first need to be *referable*. That will naturally happen over time, as you develop solid professional relationships. But without those relationships, you won't have anybody willing to write you a letter! For tactical strategies on including a recommendation letter with your job application, see chapter 3.

Possessing letters of references from current and former coworkers serves as a poignant reminder to do right by people. This suggestion seems obvious, but a bad impression can stay with someone forever.

And the world is simply too small to assume your paths won't cross again somehow. That said, if you strive to be kind and a great colleague at all times, you will continually have good people in your corner. Those are the people who will have plenty of great things to say—and write—about you.

Since graduating college, I've probably come into contact or worked with hundreds of people. Now I certainly don't expect all of those people to remember enough about me to write a letter of recommendation, or even remember me. Hopefully, if they do remember me, they won't say anything negative about my personality or work product.

At the same time, I know not everyone will like me. If you're a human being, I'd say the same applies to you. So long as you hold yourself to high standards, treat people with kindness, are consistent in your approach, and work tirelessly, you aren't *giving* other people the opportunity to speak poorly about you. They still might, but at least it's only their judgment and not something you actually did wrong.

If possible, whenever you leave a position or company, get at least one documented reference. People commonly wait until after their employment concludes to ask for a letter of recommendation. That timing certainly makes sense. Otherwise, it might seem altogether too random to ask someone for a reference if you aren't going anywhere. However, if you can muster up a bit of courage, it will behoove you to ask a trusted colleague or supervisor to write a recommendation letter while currently employed. Why? Generally, these letters turn out stronger. Imagine if someone provides you a letter of recommendation a month or two after you've departed; he or she can't actively speak to your qualifications as well as when they were literally watching you work and accomplish tasks. Also, you increase your likelihood of actually receiving a letter when you can remind your coworker about it every so often in the hallway. One time, during my last week at a job, I asked my supervisor if she could write me a letter of recommendation. More than two months after I left the company—and six follow-up emails later—she sent the letter, only to find that it was nearly identical in content to another reference I'd provided (so she could use the structure as guide). While I expressed gratitude that she took the time to follow-through, I never ended up using her letter.

At your current job, before you've given your notice, can you identify one or two individuals for whom you've developed a mutual respect? If so, see if they would be open to writing you a letter. If your reference is written by a colleague in a more superior role than your own, or by a supervisor, even better. And if they ask why you want a recommendation, you can be forthright, and mention that you came across an interesting job. On the other hand, if you don't want to jeopardize your current job by mentioning another, or you want the letter in case of a future job, you can simply say, "I recently talked to someone who said it's helpful to always have a letter of recommendation handy." You're not being deceptive; it is handy to have a reference readily available. For instance, it could be helpful for your landlord if your credit isn't sufficient. Or, if you're applying to work in a different country, any extra documentation vouching for you could help to obtain a visa. Or maybe you're thinking of applying to business school part-time. There are a number of possibilities and reasons to need a letter of recommendation outside of a job application.

CHAPTER SEVEN

LIVE IN INTUITION

"I believe in intuitions and inspirations...
I sometimes FEEL that I am right. I do not KNOW that I am."

— Albert Einstein

ACT ON YOUR "VIBES"

Our intuition is a funny thing. We all have these intangible, unexplainable senses within us, deeming certain things wrong or right, good or bad. Sometimes, we aren't even conscious of our snap judgments or feelings, yet act on them anyway. For lack of a proper term, I refer to these mysterious things as "vibes." As I see it, vibes represent the sum of an individual's senses, and together they make up one's overall intuition.

If anything in this book has resonated with you thus far, I hope it's that every individual's circumstance is situational. That's why you need to *stop doing what you should*, because there's no one prescribed way of doing or living. So how do you effectively filter through and apply all the advice you've been given thus far—including the strategies provided herein—to make it work to your advantage? By consciously and actively acting on your vibes.

Vibes are critical to your success because you can hardly ever make a decision at face value. It's nearly impossible to know everyone's motive, see all perspectives, or understand every potential implication or consequence. More importantly, sometimes there simply isn't enough time to get informed before you have to take action and make a decision.

People often underrate the value of a good gut check. Sure, you take a risk by acting solely on your vibes, but sometimes when you do, those end up being the best decisions you ever make. Every time you act on your intuition, you benefit somehow, even if you don't realize that at the time, or even years later. Regardless, the minimum benefit gained is that you alone made the choice. You empowered your future self, which can make the result of that choice easier to swallow.

When you encounter a situation that appears too good to be true, or meet someone who seems a bit threatening, your vibes ring an alarm. Our intuition sounds off all the time, even in non-threatening situations. But so rarely do people actually act on their vibes or gut instincts. Why? Most people don't know what to make of them or *how* to listen to them. They get caught up in a one-off horror story of someone they've never met who once took a risk that went awry. Or, they get lost in the advice and opinions of their elders, who often say that being spontaneous or taking guided risks isn't professionally advantageous.

To these fear-stricken folks I ask the following: If you don't listen to your instincts, then how can you identify your advantage? How can you separate yourself? If you can't dictate your own future, then aren't you the one at a *disadvantage*? Don't let your life be decided by the suggestions of others. Don't allow others' fears to become your own.

So, how do you listen to your vibes if you haven't been hearing them? First, think about where you are now. At this very moment in your life. Not yourself in the literal or geographical sense but the path you're undertaking. What step are you on in your journey? Where did you come from and how did you get to your current state of *you*?

We've all made numerous decisions along the way—some big, some small. Think about those big decisions for a bit. Mull over them. Then ask yourself, "What prompted that decision?" Maybe it was your choice of college, and you went because your dad was an alumnus. Or, maybe it was your choice of career, and your mentor thought it would be a good fit. Maybe neither of those examples applies. Whatever your path, recall and trace it, determining the root of your life's big decisions, and your actions that followed.

If your choices stem from what you thought was in your best interest at the time, it's likely you already have a solid sense of intuition. On the other hand, if your actions were taken because another prompted you, you may not be paying much attention to your intuition. Or, you might have been aware of your vibes when it came to a major decision but acted against your own gut anyway.

As you've learned, I rarely use the word "should." The term can be discouraging, as it leads one to believe that his or her fate is predetermined. If you've adopted the practice of making major decisions based on the suggestions of others, and not living in your own intuition, then you've probably predetermined your fate. But you haven't determined it, someone else has. Listening to your individual vibes is crucial so you don't regret your choices. It leads to your professional success because you feel happier when you make your passions a reality. If you happen to make a choice for your future and someone's advice falls within that course of action, all the better. That can ease your mind and support your judgment call, but your gut must still be the catalyst. Otherwise, you're only living someone else's life, and climbing his or her ladder of success.

BECOME AN "INFORMATION SEEKER"

Being well-read, or well-versed in your industry, is important for both your personal and professional advancement. If you recall, staying informed is one of the "shoulds" mentioned in chapter 1. When you aren't aware of a major event happening around you, you might look pretty foolish to friends, coworkers, neighbors, or whoever it is that knows something you don't. But there's a critical difference between keeping up with the news and seeking it out. Your intuition lies at the crux between passively staying informed and actively becoming an "information seeker."

Have you ever experienced a time when you thought you over-prepared? Or you researched something probably a little longer than necessary, or than is seemingly useful? It is in those moments when your intuition desires to become an information seeker. You may not have meant to spend so much time or effort on a particular topic, but your curiosity simply took over. The next time this happens, live in it. Don't doubt yourself, or lament about the hour you just spent exploring. Whether you actively seek out new information for your own knowledge or to share it with others, becoming an information seeker will enable endless opportunity. Here are just a few reasons why:

- **You're a source upon which others rely:** When you seek out information on your company, your coworkers gradually rely upon you for answers. There's no reason you can't become the subject-matter expert about your own organization, even if you just started! But to get there, you need to know the organization inside and out. Attend every company-wide informational or meeting. Learn every name within your own department, as well as other departments. Sit down with key employees who have witnessed the company's evolution. Going back to that silent confidence idea mentioned in chapter 6—you don't need to announce that you are a "well" of information. Eventually, once you've acquired and accumulated any information you can, offer it up in stages. Let's say that, in your research, you encountered an issue that had yet to be addressed. You, being the proactive employee that you are, volunteer to address the issue and take on this new project. If you then end up creating an incredibly useful document for your organization, you filled a need that only you knew needed to be met. You've then enabled yourself to become the de-facto expert on a particular topic, which will cause others to seek you out for answers.

- **You save others time:** Let's say you're getting lunch with a friend who mentions a new project she recently started. You, as the information seeker that you are, already know a lot about the topic. Why not extend a helping hand and inform her on what-ever you know? Since you've already put in the work, you save your friend a lot of time. Your friend will be grateful for the help, especially if she's able to put in more time on the actual project, rather than the initial time she would have spent researching.

- **You construct your own reputation:** When you can offer up tidbits that add to a conversation or enhance someone's point, people will consider you a knowledgeable or insightful person. And when you can do so in a business setting (e.g., providing a supporting statistic during your team's presentation) you construct your own reputation as an intelligent professional.

- **You create staying power:** You never know when your employer will make cuts or adjust their business model. But when you stay atop of emerging trends that relate back to your company's business, and direct your learnings to help the overall organization, you fundamentally indicate your value. If you can demonstrate how you're indispensable by keeping others informed, you thereby create staying power.

- **You give yourself a seat at the table:** When you're knowledgeable about a particular topic, people typically trust (or at least listen to) your educated comments. So when you know something that someone doesn't, and aren't afraid to share that piece of information, you present an established voice. And when you have a voice, you give yourself a seat at the table, one that others your age (or job level) may never experience.

HITTING YOUR LEARNING CEILING

Listening to your intuition is especially worthwhile when you've hit a learning ceiling at work. If you feel as though you aren't growing at the same rate in which you started, then you're only moving toward a state of dissatisfaction. At a certain point, it won't matter how great the work perks may be (e.g., you love the company, your office is located near your apartment, etc.). You can make a thousand excuses for staying in a given role, but your negative vibes will continue to tug away at you if you don't feel challenged by your daily job.

If you feel as though you've plateaued and are simply sticking with the status quo, live in—and act on—your intuition. Remember that your professional success is dependent upon your personal happiness, so identify whether there are any changes you can make at work to help you feel greater satisfaction. Can you take on different responsibilities in some capacity? Can you have a conversation with your manager and explain to him or her that you'd like an opportunity to further develop your skill set? Express that you'd like to work on something fresh to provide you with a new perspective.

Others are also following in the intuition revolution. In a study published by the Harvard Business Review, learning is one of two essential factors that contributes to an employee's success in his/her job. The other? Vitality.[2] If you aren't excited or passionate about going into work anymore because you are no longer learning, you *owe* it to yourself to make a change.

IT'S NOT ALL ABOUT THE MONEY

That same Harvard study indicated another surprising fact about job satisfaction: It's not all about the money. I wholeheartedly agree; it's really not. For instance, when I'm interviewing for a job, I'll never bring up the word "money" until the interviewer does. It's an awful feeling when you dislike a job or a company. For that reason, I prefer to hear about the position first and any potential growth opportunities before I receive the company's financial offer.

I also don't bring money up in an initial interview because it can sound presumptuous, as if I've already been granted a second round interview *during* my first interview. It's important to think about the perspective of the interviewer. If they're simply trying to glean whether or not you have the skill set to be successful in the position, they might be deterred if you're negotiating salary with them before you've even proved that you are capable.

Also, you never know when you'll be in contact with someone again, or who that recruiter/hiring manager knows. If you bring up money too early into a conversation, that will likely stand out to your interviewer more than anything else that was said. You might have really great experience, but if your focus seems to be primarily about the money, this may actually make you appear inexperienced, as it is common knowledge to not be the first person to mention money.

Moreover, you don't know the company's budget. If you wait until your interviewer mentions salary, and you're a bit farther along in the interview process, the company might meet your salary requirements. Regardless of pay, it can't hurt to learn more about a company or position if it seemed initially interesting. Money shouldn't always be the deciding factor in pursuing a new job. If it's a considerable pay cut that could potentially impact your personal happiness, then maybe entertaining the position isn't realistic. But if the job could potentially provide you more professional happiness *now*, is only a small dock in pay, and comes with great growth potential, it might be worthwhile to consider.

Assuming you've waited until the interviewer mentions salary, what's your response when they do? At most corporations, the question asked is, "What are your salary expectations?" One possible response is providing a salary range that still leaves some room for negotiation. A reasonable response to this question might be, "The compensation for positions where I've interviewed fall within X to Y range, so I'd ideally like to make something comparable. But I am open to hearing more about the role, even if that compensation doesn't fit your requirements." Any similar response illustrates maturity and open-mindedness. If I ever provide a specific figure, I always state a value about 8–12 percent higher than my current salary. If you're paid on the low end, a 10 percent hike is a fair value. If you don't know what a fair salary for your position might be, go to a website like Glassdoor, which provides average market salaries according to job title, region, and experience. I've had colleagues and/or mentors tell me hiring managers assume that 10 percent hike nowadays, and to opt for 30 percent instead. Personally, that makes me uncomfortable, but listen to your intuition. It's your money, after all. Regardless of whether it's your first or fifth time, a salary negotiation is never an easy conversation.

WHEN GENDER MATTERS

Our intuition also plays a key role whenever we sense discrimination in the workplace. While I could discuss discrimination against race, sexual orientation, religion, or other identifiers, I'm going to focus on gender here, as it's the differentiator I most relate with in my career.

Despite being a female sportswriter for a few years, the only time I had an inkling of gender discrimination wasn't at that job. Players in the locker room are actually more respectful than you'd think. Note: Some can still be pigs, but that isn't isolated to the workplace. More often, it was actually male media members who were inappropriate, rather than the athletes themselves.

No, I did not encounter discrimination when I was a member of the media. This incident occurred years later. I was penalized for being a woman ever so subtly, but it hit a tipping point at a weeklong work event. As evident in this book, my natural inclination when I meet new people is to look for shared interests, whether the person is a man or woman. At this event, I was required to communicate frequently with several senior executives of another company. Because most of our work happened in real-time, these executives commonly communicated with us via cell phone. We typically saw them throughout the day, and sometimes in the evenings for parties related to the larger event. They often communicated their needs or ideas through me, or one of my bosses. After the event concluded, I arrived back home feeling pretty confident about the role I played in strengthening our relationship with this partner. Unfortunately, I was alone in that mindset. I began to sense my first dose of gender discrimination when my manager suggested that I hadn't maintained a professional relationship with a couple of these executives. Funny enough, I had taken extra precautions with these individuals to avoid that very accusation! I triple-checked the appropriateness of my text messages or emails, and I was often the designated driver for our eight-person team. Whenever I wasn't driving, I never consumed more than two drinks. Since the event concluded, I have shown the communications to others outside my team, and everyone except my manager and his boss, both men, believes I maintained my professionalism. Never once did I question or feel uncomfortable at these executives' outreach. Ultimately, the disagreement with my boss forever altered our work relationship, and I quit a short time thereafter. I truly feel in this instance that if I were a man and had taken the exact same actions, I would have been praised rather than punished. Despite my departure from the company, I still have a great business relationship with those executives. They have been valuable resources in my career.

Sometimes, discrimination also exists within our own gender. In my parents' generation, if a woman went out to dinner with a married man—regardless of whether she was also married—the woman was thought to be doing something inappropriate. This stereotype still has legs today (pun intended), even if the two only discuss work and their rapport is strictly professional. For example, because I've traveled a lot in my career, I have a few advisors who live in other states. If they are visiting my state on business and happen to be free, but only at dinnertime, I'm not going to turn down the opportunity to meet this person because I'm a woman and he's a man— and it's past 5pm. I see this meeting as an opportunity to learn and strengthen my business relationship. This is another instance when our intuition plays a key role in our professional decisions: If I sense that the other person is cordial, respectful, and professional, then I'll let my good vibes be my guide and disregard what others might think. At the same time, it is extremely important to be wary of the message you send *your contact*. A few of the more obvious indicators that you aren't maintaining your professionalism include drinking too much alcohol (most would argue more than two glasses) during a business meeting or function, not splitting the bill, or wearing something too revealing.

If you're an attractive female, it's easy to be swayed by men in business. But the moment you lose your self-respect, the other person has lost respect for you, too. You may encounter many forked roads on your climb to professional satisfaction and prosperity. Where will your intuition lead you? Ask yourself the following questions: "Will I take the easier of these two roads and flirt with, or succumb, to successful males' advances, in order to reach new career heights? Or, "Will I take the arguably lesser-paved road, where I take advantage of these unique opportunities and meetings only to showcase my skill set, or discuss business objectives in the hopes of future collaboration?" Only you can make that call. But before you decide, remember to be confident in your most valuable asset, which happens to be gender-neutral: your mind.

"Everything will not work out as initially planned. It might work out as well as you imagined, but it will definitely work out differently."

Lastly, we can also discriminate against our advisors. While I've generally found men to be more receptive to offering advice—likely because I work in a male-dominated industry—I've received equally valuable advice from women. Be sure to seek out advice from reputable people, regardless of gender. Learn from whomever you can, whenever you can.

Hopefully this book demonstrates the importance of listening to, and living in, your intuition. Trusting your gut throughout everything you do is critical to your development, as it helps guide your decisions and discerns "right" from "wrong." Think of your intuition as your personal "Should Barometer." While you can't quantitatively measure intuition (although some have tried[12]), your instincts can guide you to decide whether you "should" make this or that choice.

Regardless of how you arrive at a given decision, you're still bound to make mistakes. Everything will not work out as initially planned. It might work out *as well* as you imagined, but it will definitely work out differently. Let your vibes be your ultimate guide rather than planning every detail along the way. And don't fret when things don't take their "proper" course. You will undoubtedly stumble along the way and regret a decision or two. Even if you try to avoid making them, mistakes still happen. Celebrate them, because when you follow your instincts, the sum of your failures will always be less than the sum of your successes.

---

[12] www.coll.mpg.de/DOWNLOAD/intuitiveexperts/pdf/workshop%20on%20measuring%20intuition%20and%20expertise%20%20abstracts.pdf

CHAPTER EIGHT

TAKE THE PLUNGE

"Never confuse movement with action."

- Ernest Hemingway

NOW THAT WE'VE DISCUSSED what you should do, as well as when to abolish "should," the next step is putting these tactics into motion. Which, if any, of these chapters have resonated with you? Where can you incite action in your life or career? Where can you take the plunge?

Your end goal is personal and professional happiness, right? Without taking a risk, or applying any of the against-the-grain tactics discussed, you can't really grasp what the "happiest" version of you looks like. Instead, you're simply accepting the status quo, rather than changing it.

All of the approaches detailed herein won't necessarily work for you. You might even regret heeding some of them. But remember they are merely suggestions—I didn't say you *should* follow them. These tips are meant to help empower you and your future, not force you onto any one path.

EMERGING JOB FLEXIBILITY

In the last 15 years, the job market has shifted dramatically. We live in the digital golden age, where more startups exist (and can survive) than ever before.[13] In fact, small businesses, defined as a business with fewer than 500 employees, have generated over 65 percent of the overall American workforce since 1995[14] and about 50 percent of those businesses survive for at least five years.[15] Because of the Internet boom and the emergence of diversified skill sets, we've become less dependent on major corporations to make ends meet than when our parents were at the peak of their careers.

Now, your livelihood is customizable, tailored to fit your individual schedule, passions, and strengths. With this job flexibility comes versatility: We can work almost anywhere we want, in practically any field we desire. Working at one place for more than a few years is considered a rarity these days; staying in the same industry for your entire career is even rarer. If you want options, take them. There's no better time than the present. Change your career if you're unsure, or ask for a new role if you're feeling stagnant. Whatever your move, determine your reason for making it and then do it. Deciding to make a change may impact your personal development, more than the result of the change itself. When you've decided to make a change for yourself, you are living your life the way you imagined it, not the way others say you should.

[13] www.linkedin.com/pulse/20131210124302-758147-big-idea-2014-an-unprecedented-explosion-in-startups
[14] www.forbes.com/sites/jasonnazar/2013/09/09/16-surprising-statistics-about-small-businesses/
[15] www.sba.gov/sites/default/files/FAQ_Sept_2012.pdf

MAKE YOURSELF INVALUABLE

In the beginning of this book, I included a list of tactics that one "should" reasonably follow, or when it's in your best interest to adhere to "should" advice. I have one more to add to the list, but this "should" isn't as straightforward as proofreading your emails or sending a follow-up note. This "should" is a skill in and of itself because it's up for individual interpretation. Honestly, it's probably the most important advice I've received that I also try to adopt daily: the art of making yourself invaluable.

I call the skill an "art" because, if everyone could accomplish it, then competition would cease to exist. If we all possessed endless value to someone or something, then few would leave their current positions. The impact of being invaluable also extends to our personal lives; nobody would ever break up with us nor would our landlord ever increase the rent! If we were truly invaluable at work, we'd also be indispensable. We'd likely receive fair compensation, earn the respect of our peers and superiors, and be treated well. Sounds like a professional dream come true!

Maybe you've heard this advice before. Or maybe it's your first time. Either way, the reminder in and of itself holds value: Being invaluable gives you staying power. And while it is a skill that everyone "should" strive to possess, whether or not you're *actually* valuable is dependent upon someone else's opinion. Still, here are a couple approaches you can take that might help other people see you as invaluable:

Respond quickly. Whether you're setting up a meeting with a new contact or coordinating an internal team session, effective communication is critical. What is invaluable about being an effective communicator is that others then find you reliable. While it's a wonderful reprieve to leave your phones at home every once in a while, if you're in the middle of your work week or in mid-correspondence with someone, you must do your utmost to close the loop. Why is this constant communication important? Because most people don't consider *the other person.* What if he or she is waiting on your response before scheduling a separate appointment? If you always keep the other person in mind—be it your boss, friend, business contact, landlord, etc.—then your communications will reflect that, and others will see you as a reliable communicator. It seems a rather basic premise, but you'd be surprised at how many people are sporadic communicators, relaying messages on their own time. Sometimes intermittent communication is a pride thing, where one or both parties don't want to respond immediately and thus appear available. Forget all that and set aside your ego. If I've seen and responded to your email two minutes ago, chances are I've also seen your response that you sent thirty seconds ago. In that case, I'm going to respond right away to wrap up our correspondence.

Offer help. Offering to help someone can go a long way in cementing a relationship. We're often so quick to take rather than give: We seek the advice of others, all the while asking for job referrals and recommendations, drinking at the well until only droplets remain. But from my conversations with people over the years, it seems that those who give the most—and offer to give first—usually end up receiving more than their output. The key is to give to someone else without any expectation of a return. Helping others is not a recipe for reciprocity. We help to become invaluable, dependable, someone's confidant, or "trusted soldier." As millennials, you might not have much to offer your business contacts yet, but that's expected. That said, hopefully you still at least offer to help. Even if you can't offer anything of tangible value, leave a conversation saying, "If there is anything I can ever do for you, please name it." But only say such a thing if you actually mean it. And when that day comes and you follow through on your words, your conscientiousness demonstrates your value.

"We're often so quick to take rather than give: We seek the advice of others, all the while asking for job referrals and recommendations, drinking at the well until only droplets remain."

Tie yourself to revenue. To get your boss or supervisor to believe you are invaluable, you have to first show them what you can bring in *real value*. What aspects of the business are you touching or working on that can lead to an increased profit margin? Could you argue that your work improved those margins? If your work isn't affected by revenue, what does your team care about? In preparation for your quarterly or yearly review, identify whatever roles, responsibilities, or projects you took on that produced numbers of any kind. If you can show you worked on X and that somehow (even if indirectly) led to the financial result of Z, you added value. Another way to look at this is to pinpoint how your work *saved* the company money. Did you assess the value of X and demonstrate to your team why X doesn't make financial sense in the long-term? Or, did you work on some part of a negotiation that led to a bigger gain, without much expense on your company's end? That's all value. Demonstrate any revenue correlation that you can, and then document it.

Make your boss look good. We all think about ourselves more than anyone else. But another way to prove you are invaluable to your boss is by determining what's in it for them. From your time spent working together, can you identify his or her individual goals? If not, can you be forthright and ask? Once you ascertain—or at least gain a clearer idea of—their goals, can you impact his or her growth in some fashion? Can you take work off his or her plate? Can you look for a creative solution to a problem they are trying to solve? Can you take the blame in a situation, which could have been caused by their poor communication or direction? Can you bring him or her lunch when they are having a busy day? Look for ways to make your boss' life easier. We tend to focus so much on how we can get promoted, rather than on how we get people to *want* to promote us. When we focus on the latter, including how to make our bosses look good, we actually end up helping ourselves.

SHOW PASSION!

I'll leave you with one final recommendation, as it's the topic I found most surprising. In all of my research for this book—including meeting with several recruiters and reading nearly a hundred career-related articles—I encountered one common trait that employers said most job seekers lacked: passion.[16] How can this be? Why are you even at an interview if you are not the least bit excited about the position? Better yet, if you aren't enthusiastic about working for that company, you're sending a message to the hiring manager that *they* shouldn't be enthusiastic about you, either.

If you learn or adopt nothing from this book but to show more passion in your life, I'll consider my endeavor a success. We are given one life. Why be anything but passionate?

Hopefully, if you weren't already passionate, you can seek out an extra pep to your step to recharge your motor. What often works for me is viewing every Monday as the first day at a new job. Sounds silly, but it helps me approach each week with newfound excitement. Find what works best for you, and go on and live that passionate life! Take the plunge. And do so with as much passion as you can muster.

---

[16] www.emc.com/collateral/article/100-job-search-tips.pdf

CHAPTER NINE

ONE-OFF "SHOULDS"

"Luck is the residue of design."

- Branch Rickey

BELOW IS A COLLECTION of random "should" advice I've received over the years. While you may have heard similar guidance, I've included these quotes because they helped light a fire when I needed it, or made me think about something in a different way. I hope you find them as thought-provoking.

"Be yourself. It's your best selling point."
– John Black, Vice President of Public Relations, Los Angeles Lakers

"If people want to tell you things, you can connect with anybody. It's not a strength everyone has but if you can possess it, it will carry you in whatever path you choose."
– George Whitfield, CEO Whitfield Athletix

"Keep talking with people about their career paths and eventually, the right opportunity will illuminate."
– Robert Perile, Partner, Shamrock Capital Advisors

"The position you want might not be listed, but keep putting yourself out there anyway. The job you want may turn up in the connections you make."
– Gary Klein, Writer, Los Angeles Times

"As long as you maintain your sincerity, people won't assume you have ulterior motives."
– Jeff Fellenzer, Professor, USC Annenberg School for Communication and Journalism

"Acknowledge your strengths without selling them."
– Gary Rudnick, President, Americas at Golin Harris

"When your authenticity comes through, people will want to do business with you."
– Forrest Dorsett, CEO, Dorsett Sports Marketing

"Starting off your career and building it into something takes an incredible amount of patience. You are a rookie. Expect to carry the helmets for a long time."
– Marcellus Wiley, Former NFL Player, Current ESPN Analyst

"Look for all sides of something. Try to find the thing that nobody is thinking or talking about."
– David Schwab, Managing Director, Octagon First Call

"Follow the four Cs: confidence, competence, character and compassion and anything you do will come out with class."
– Lorenzo Neal, Former NFL Player, Current Broadcaster

"Instead of competing with your peers, learn from them."
– Jeff Su, CTO, Second Spectrum

"Remember: stop, breathe, and smell the roses."
– David Miyabe, Art Director, Second Spectrum

CPSIA information can be obtained at www.ICGtesting.com
Printed in the USA
LVOW07s0121170216

475348LV00003B/230/P